SUNFLOWERS

by Patricia Burke

ISBN- 13: 978-1-951576-01-1

Cover Art by Hand Drawn by Doodle Artist Patricia Burke
Cover Art- Colored by Debbie West Cummings

Patricia Burke would love to see your colored version of her art.
You can find her here:

http://coloradoodle.com
https://www.facebook.com/coloradoodle/
https:// www.facebook.com/groups/

Join the official fan group here;
facebook.com/groups/colornydoodles.patriciaburke

~SUNFLOWERS~

Coloring Team

Brenda Hanson
Cari McBroom Jimenez
Charlotte Schroeder Beeston
Debbie West Cummings
Dee Dee Boseman
Jennifer Knisely Preston
Kelly Deuber Taylor
Patricia Jingle
Susan Nicita
Vicki Ardito

I would like to dedicate this coloring book to these amazing ladies who spend their time coloring whatever I throw at you.
Good or not, your enthusiasm, has encouraged me to keep going. Without this tiny group of amazing women, this journey would not be near as fun as it is.
For your honesty, sharp eyes and good humor, I thank you.
Patricia

THIS BOOK BELONGS TO

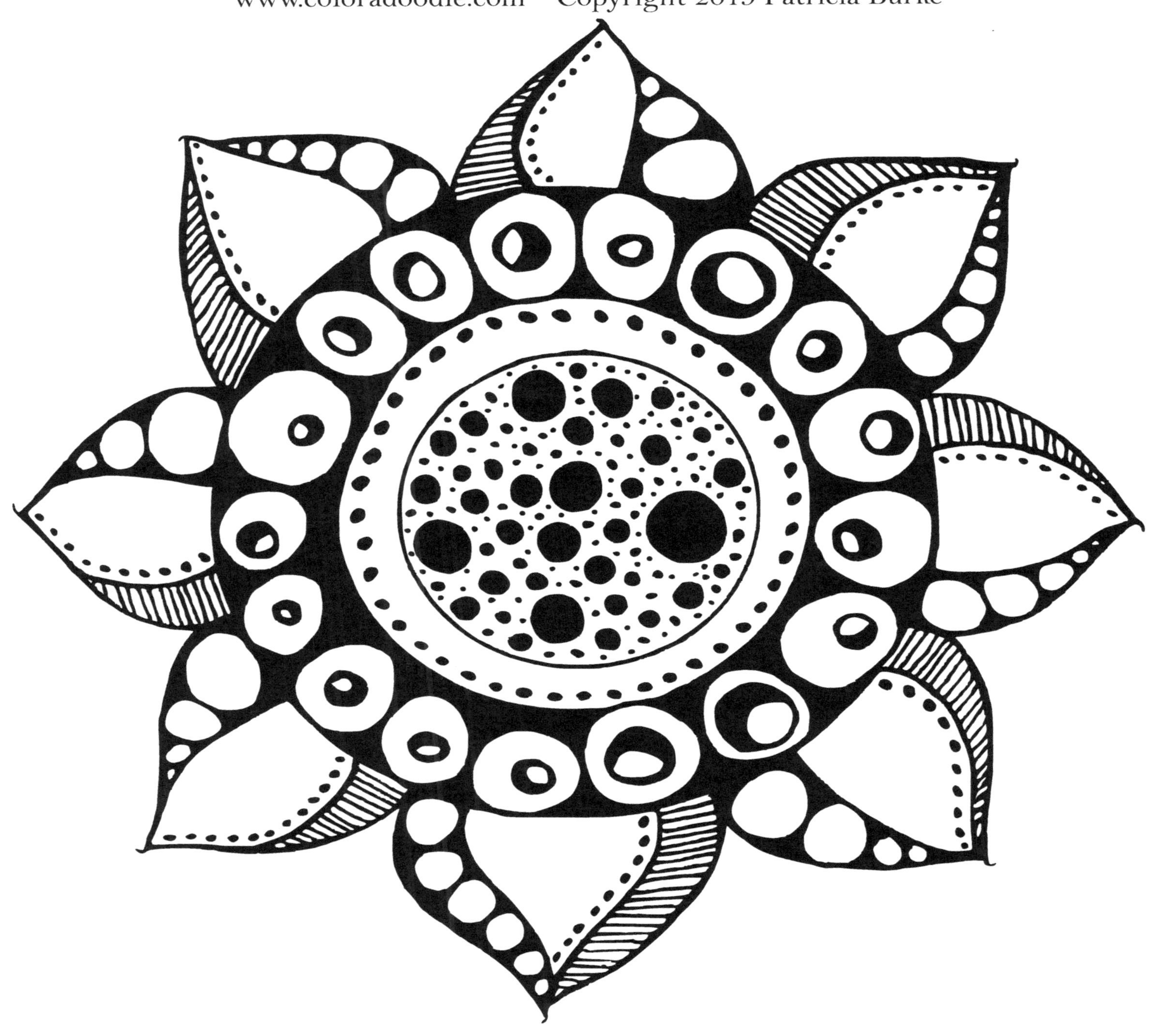

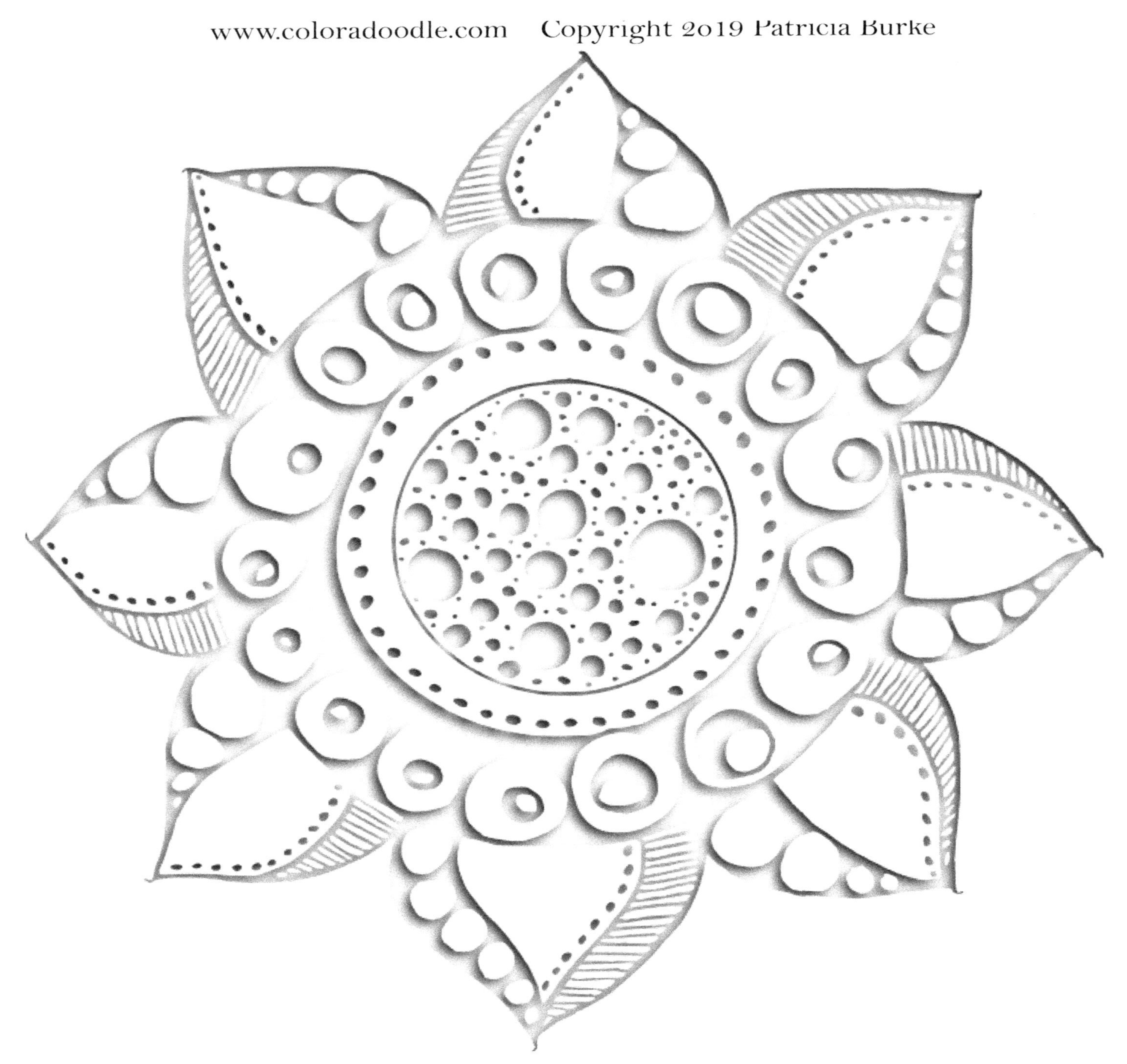

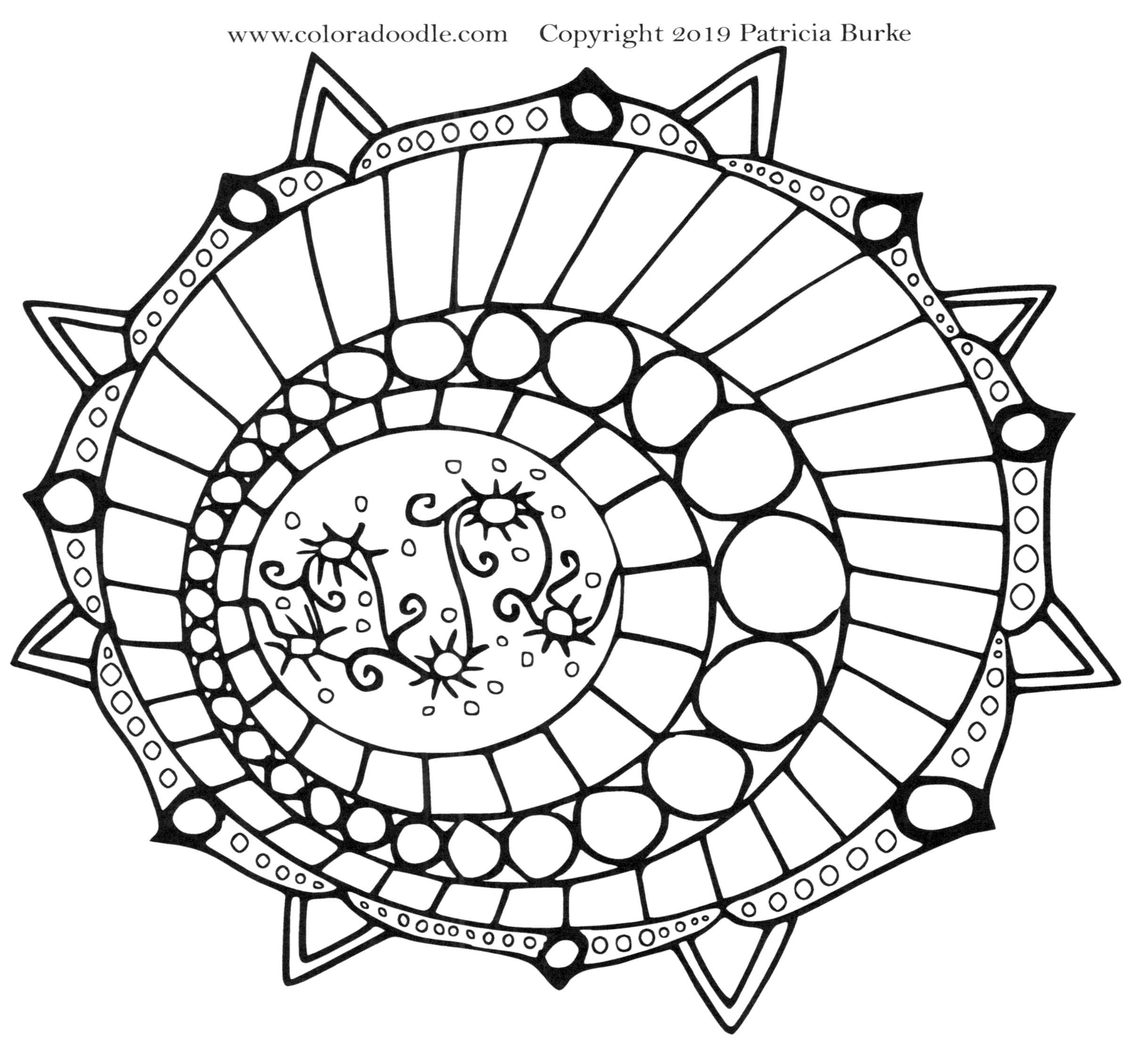

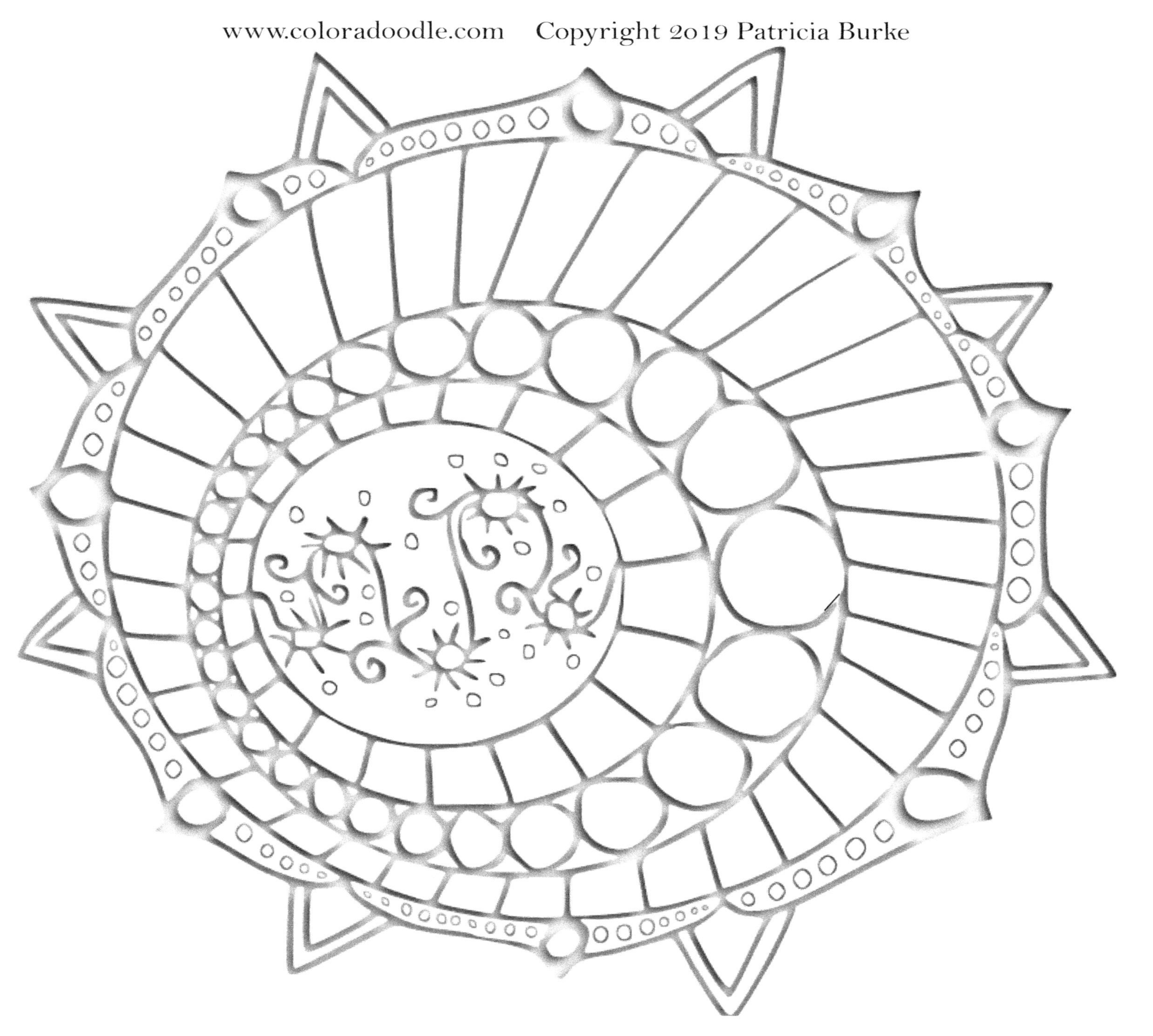

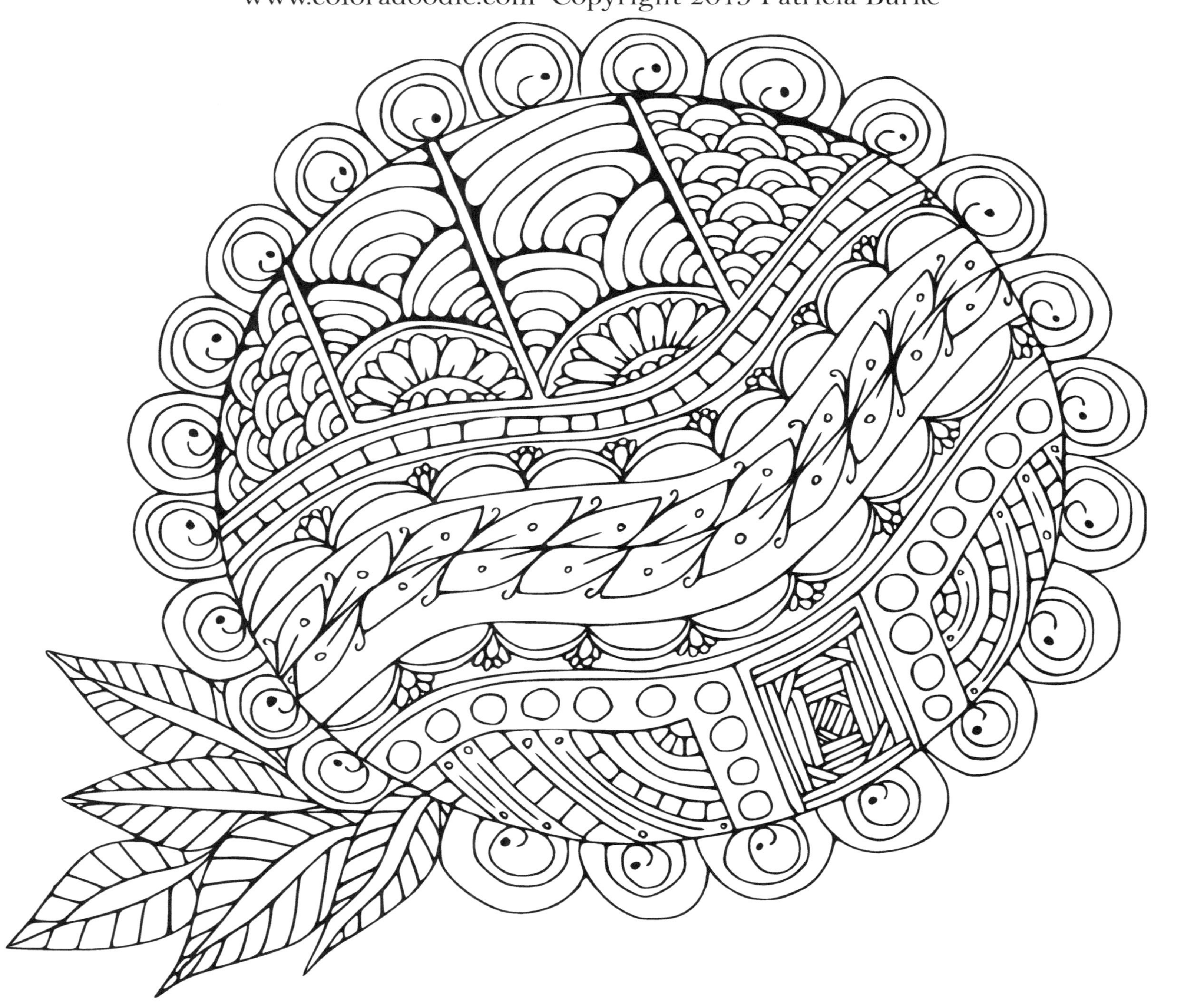

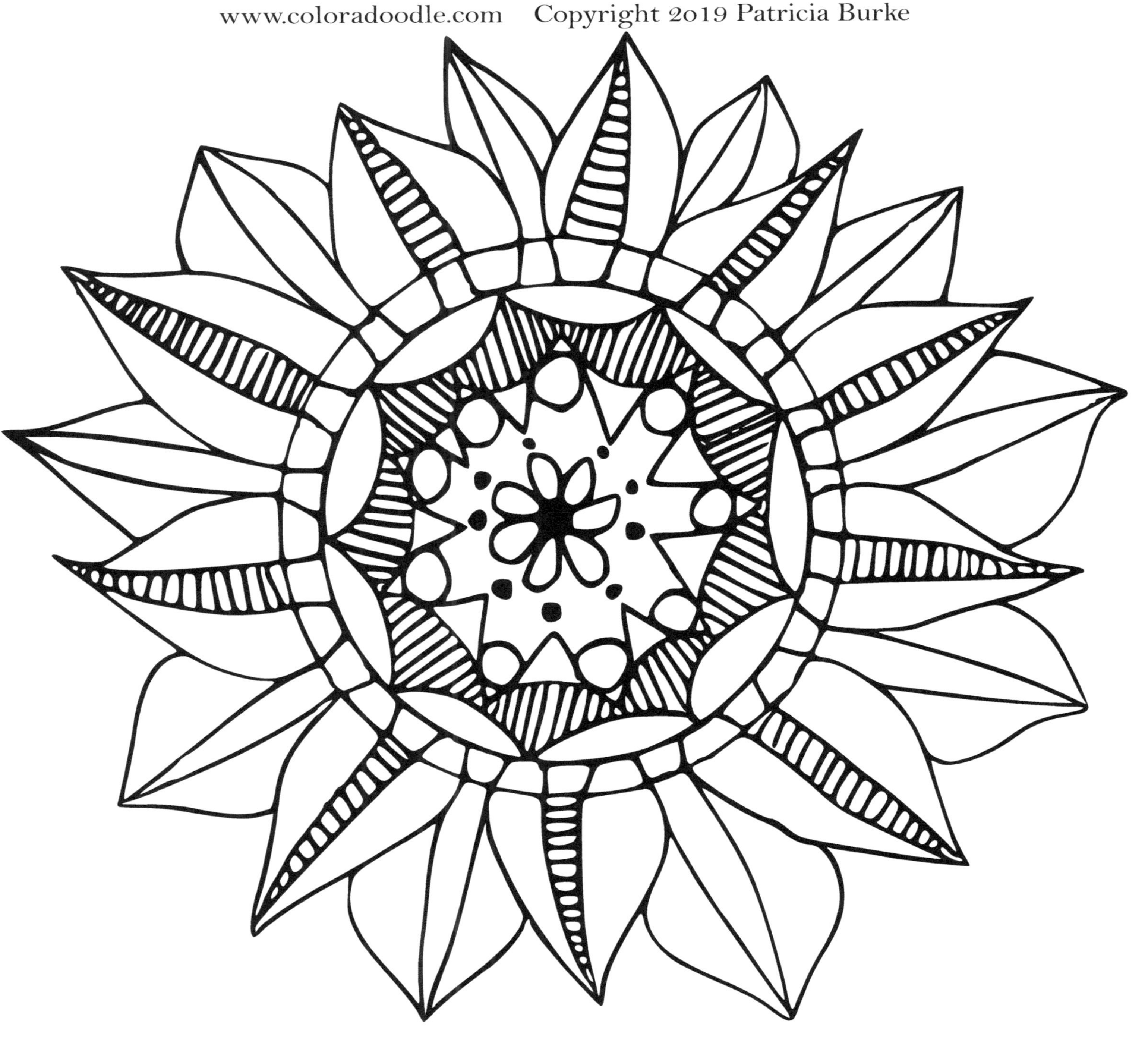

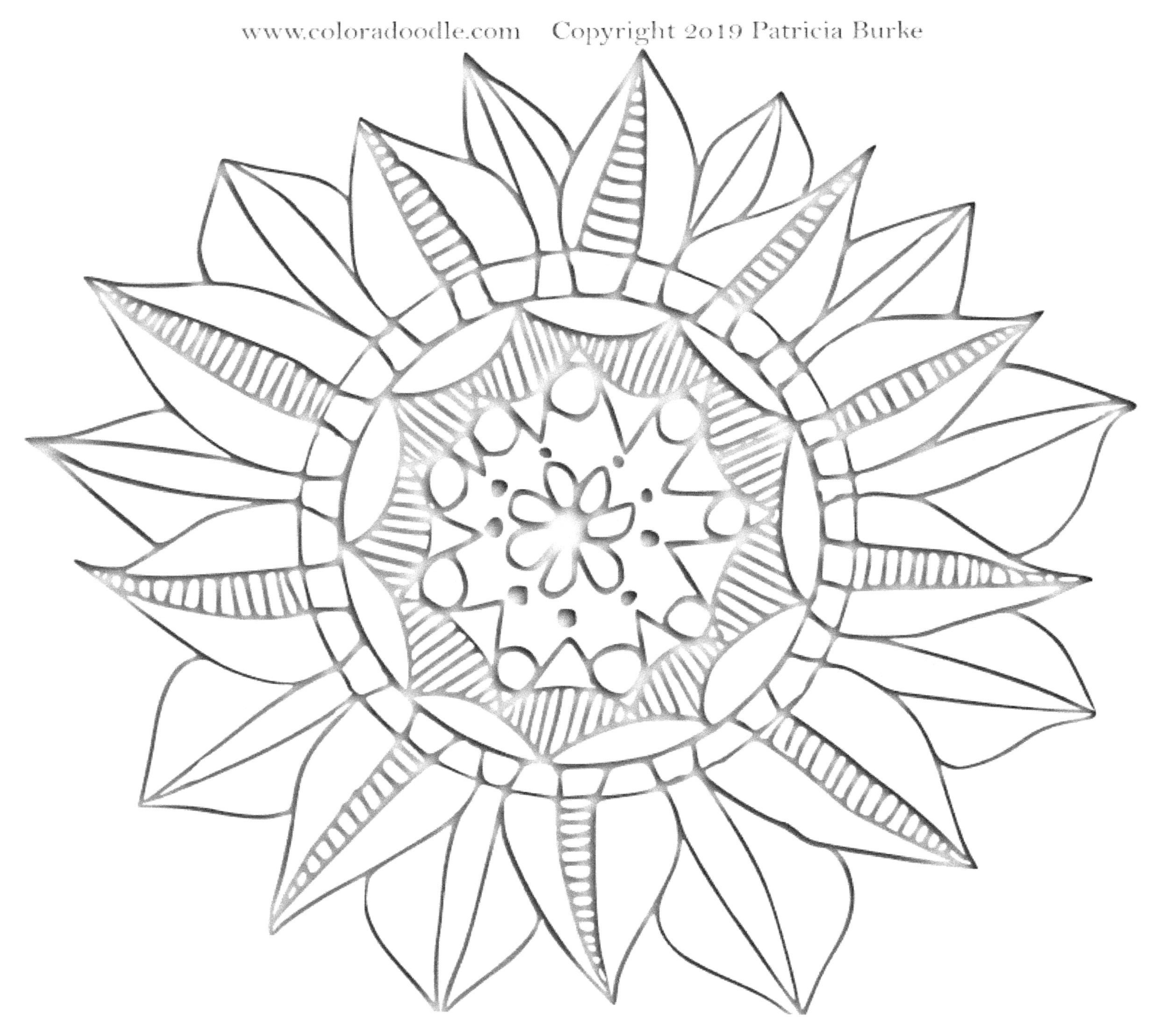

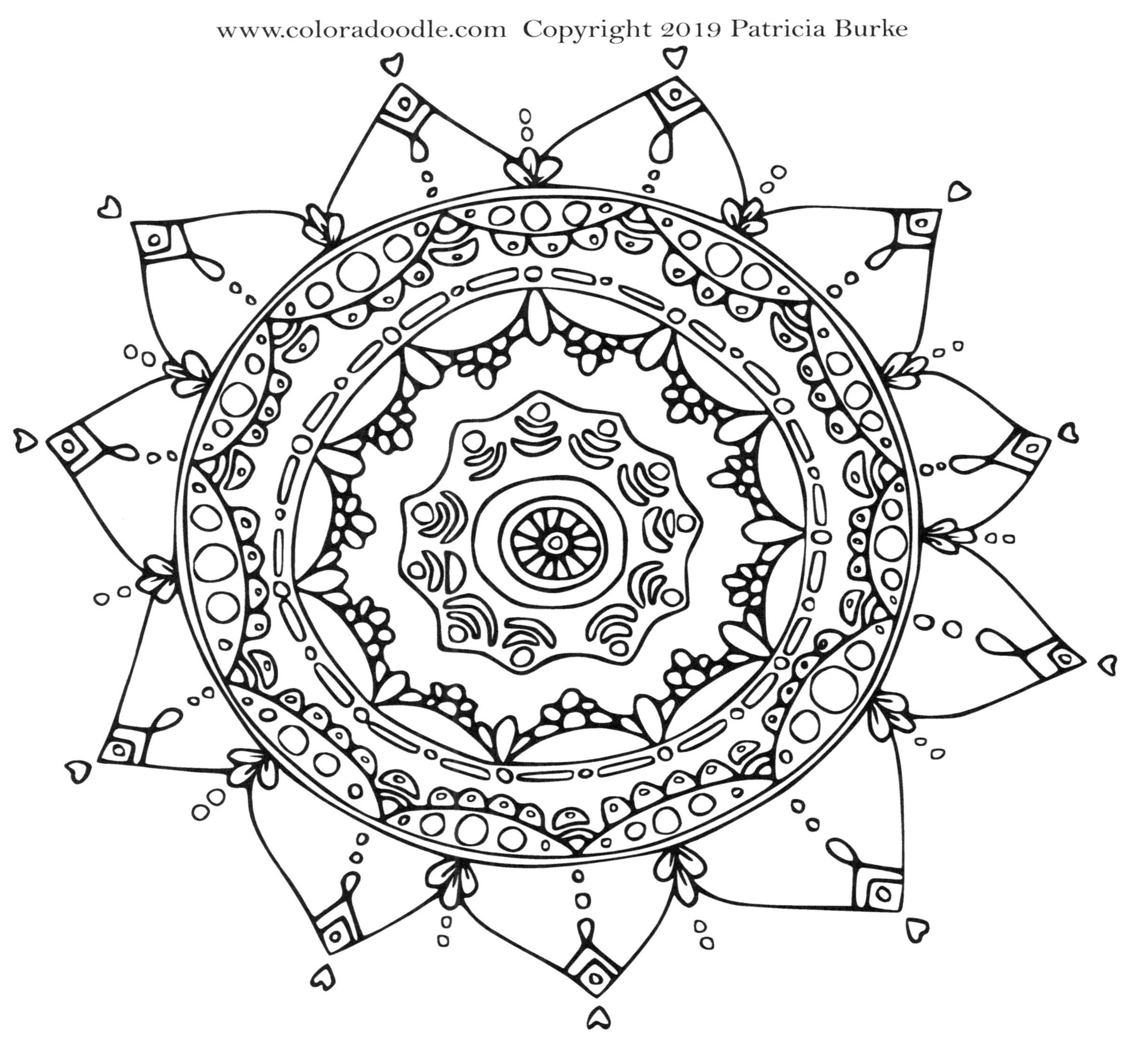

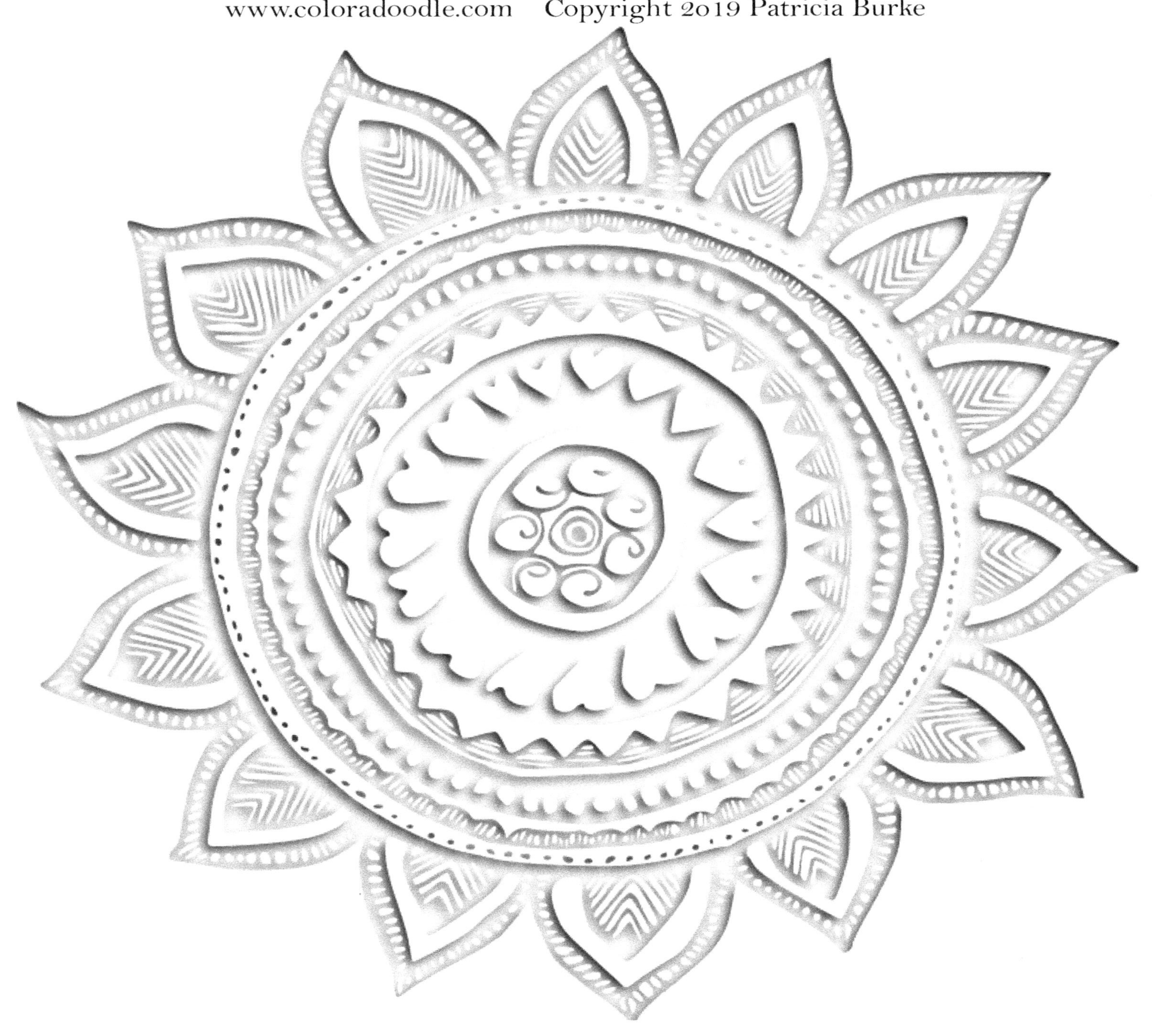

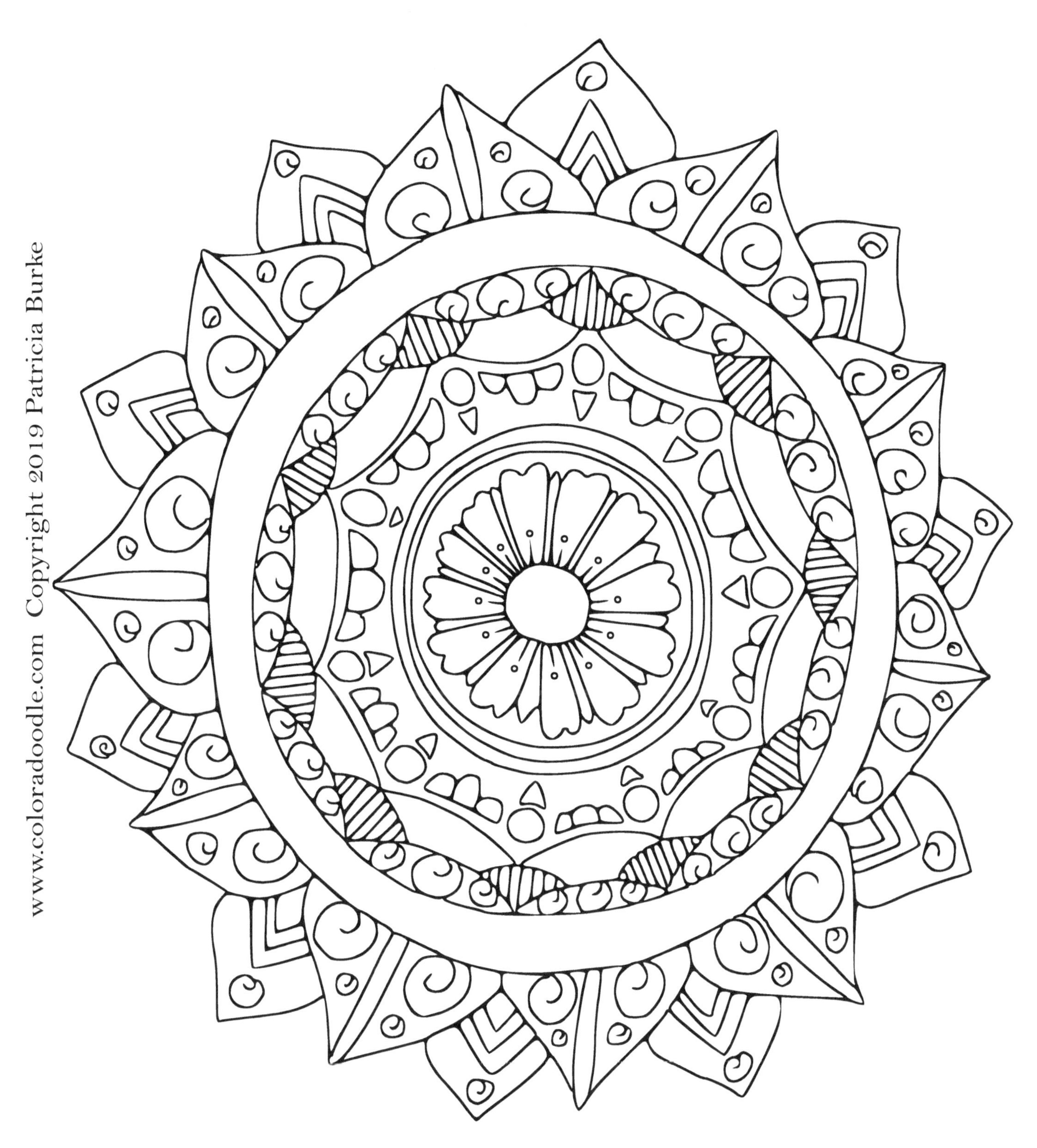

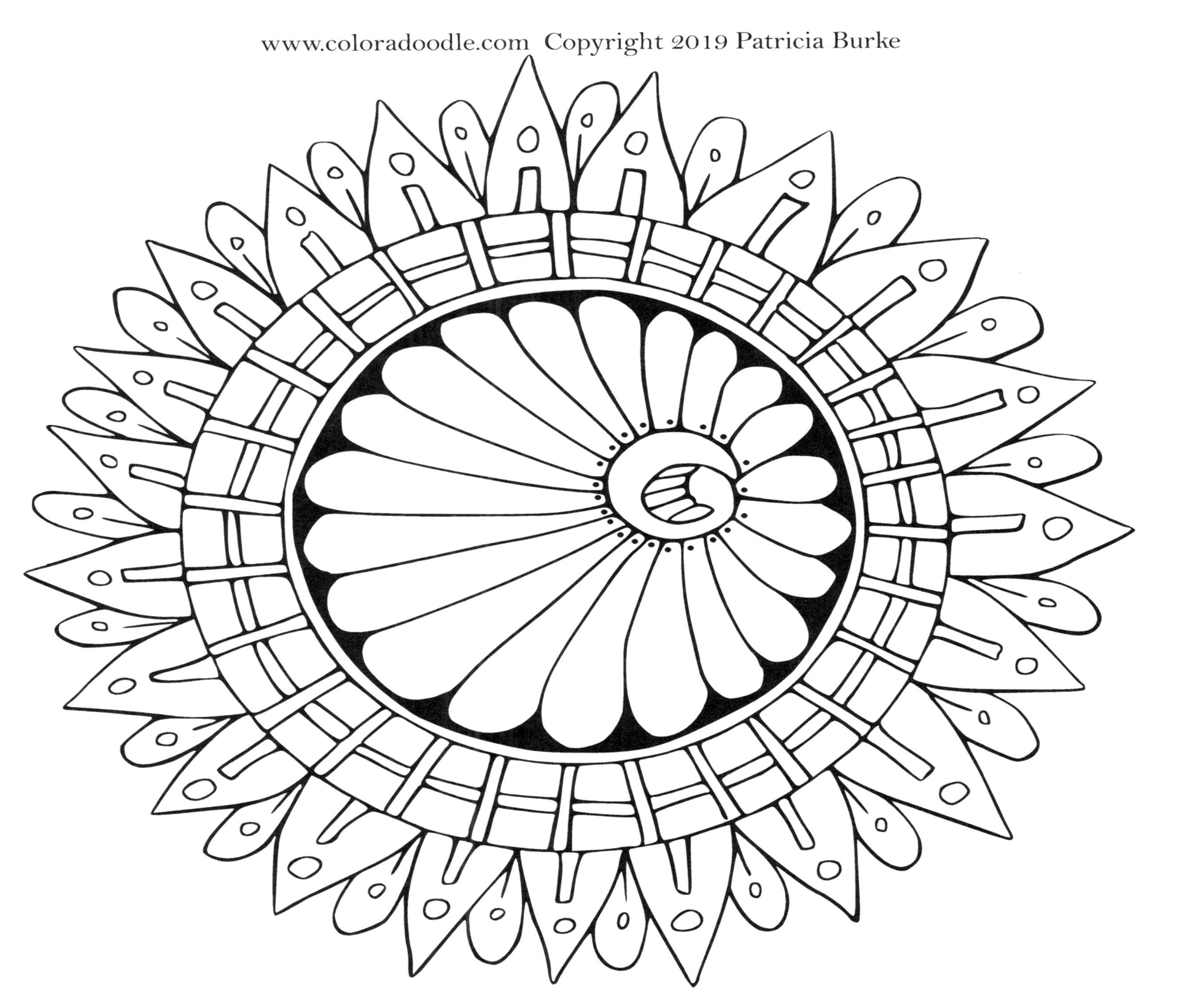

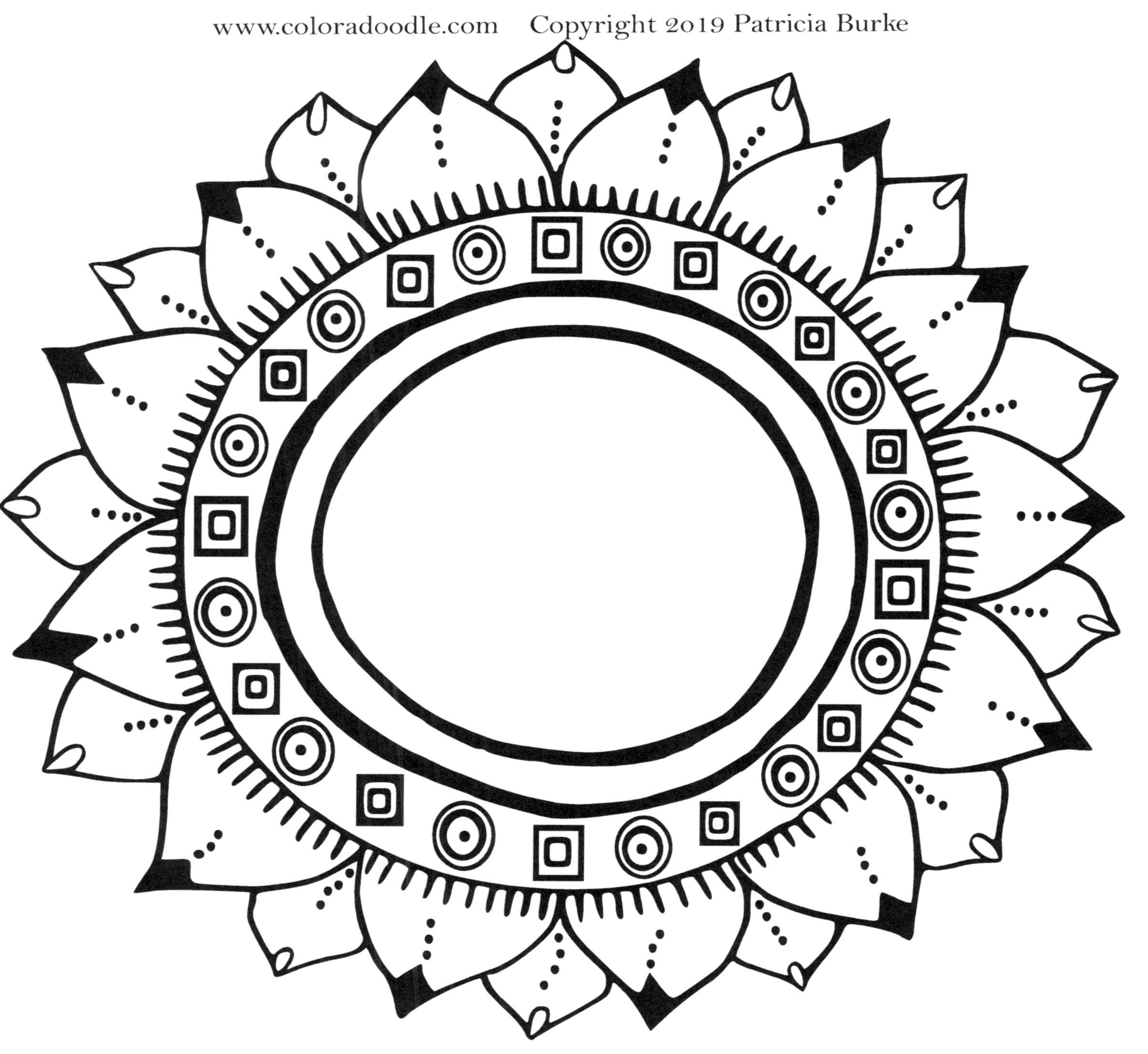

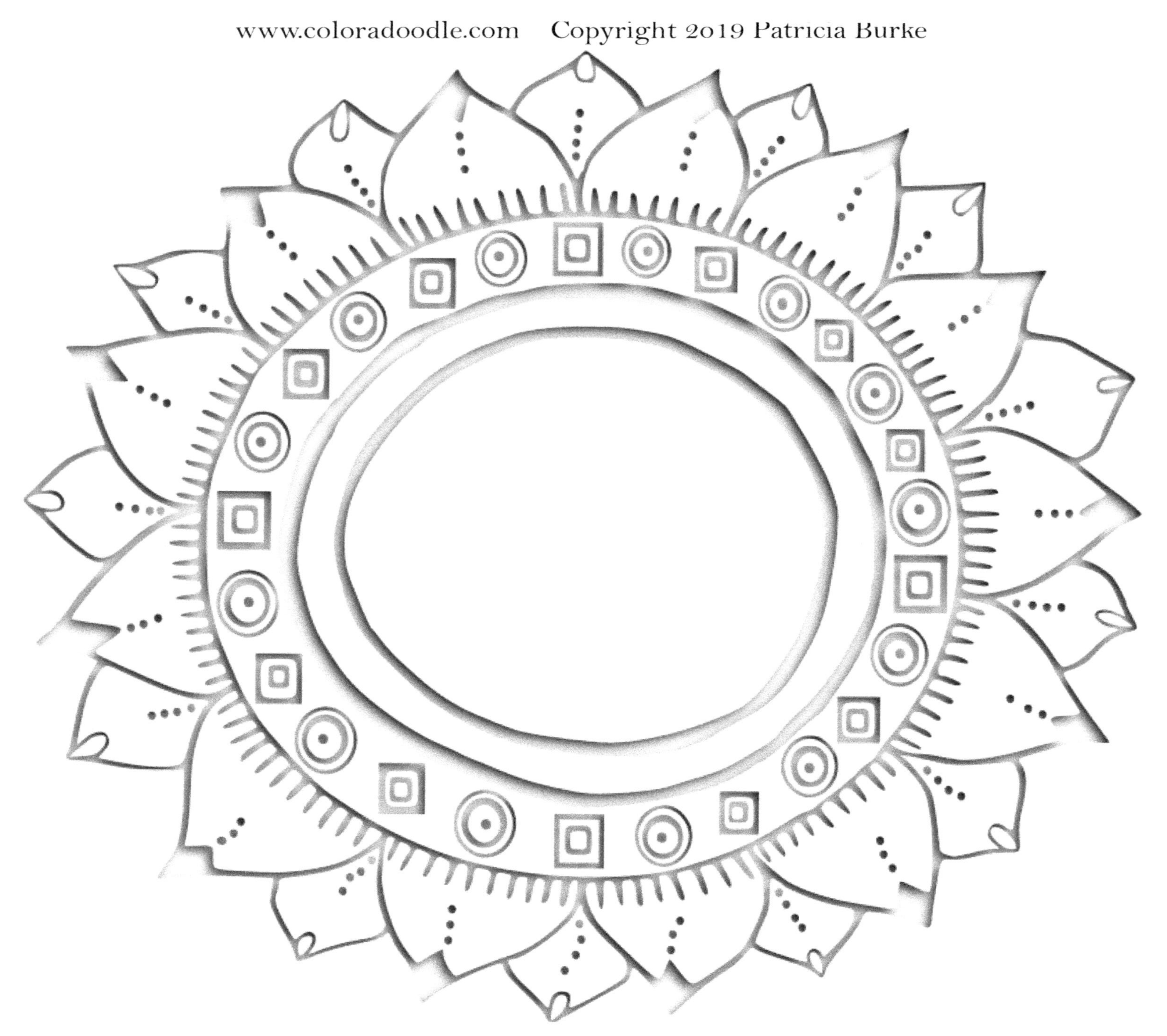

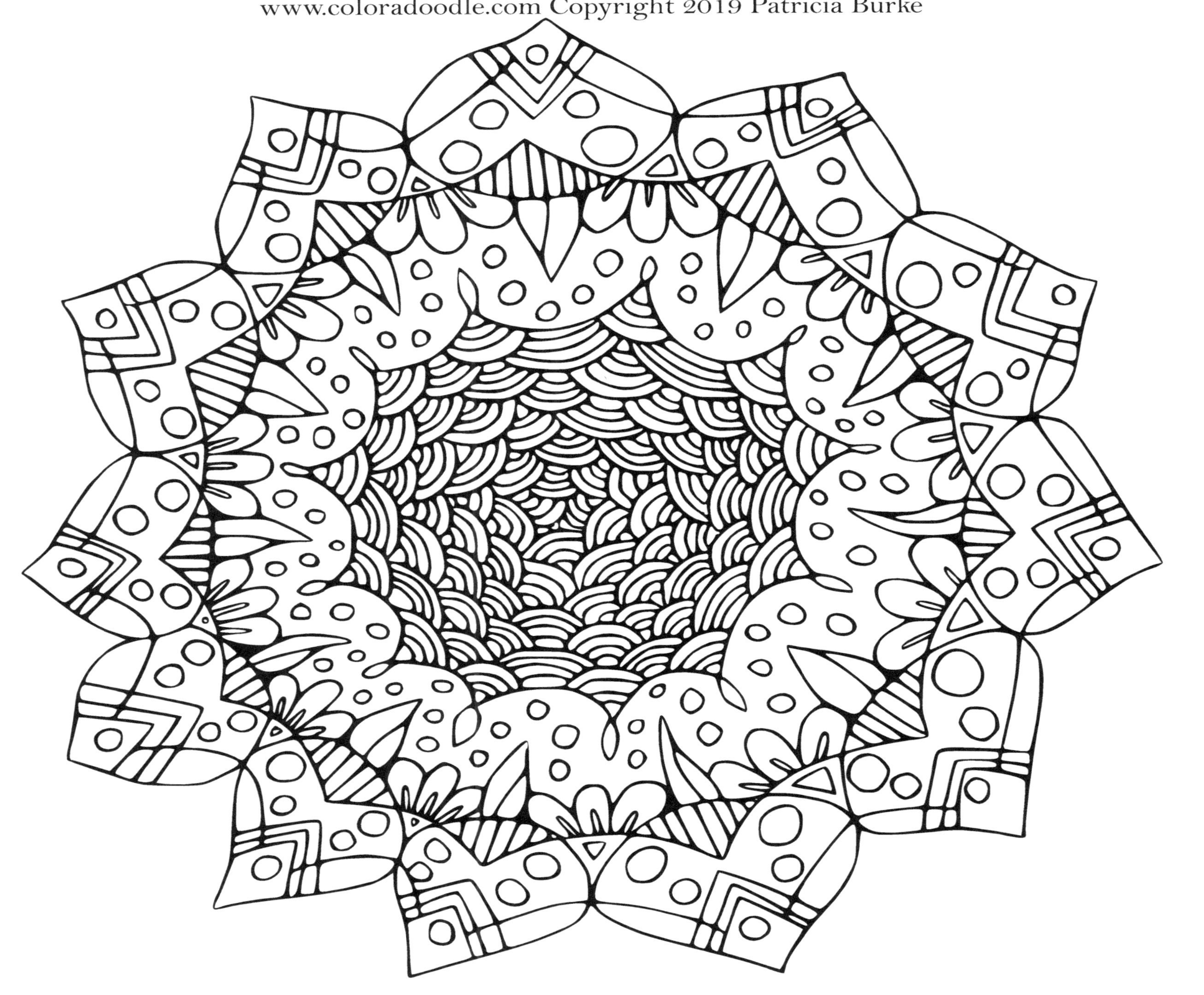

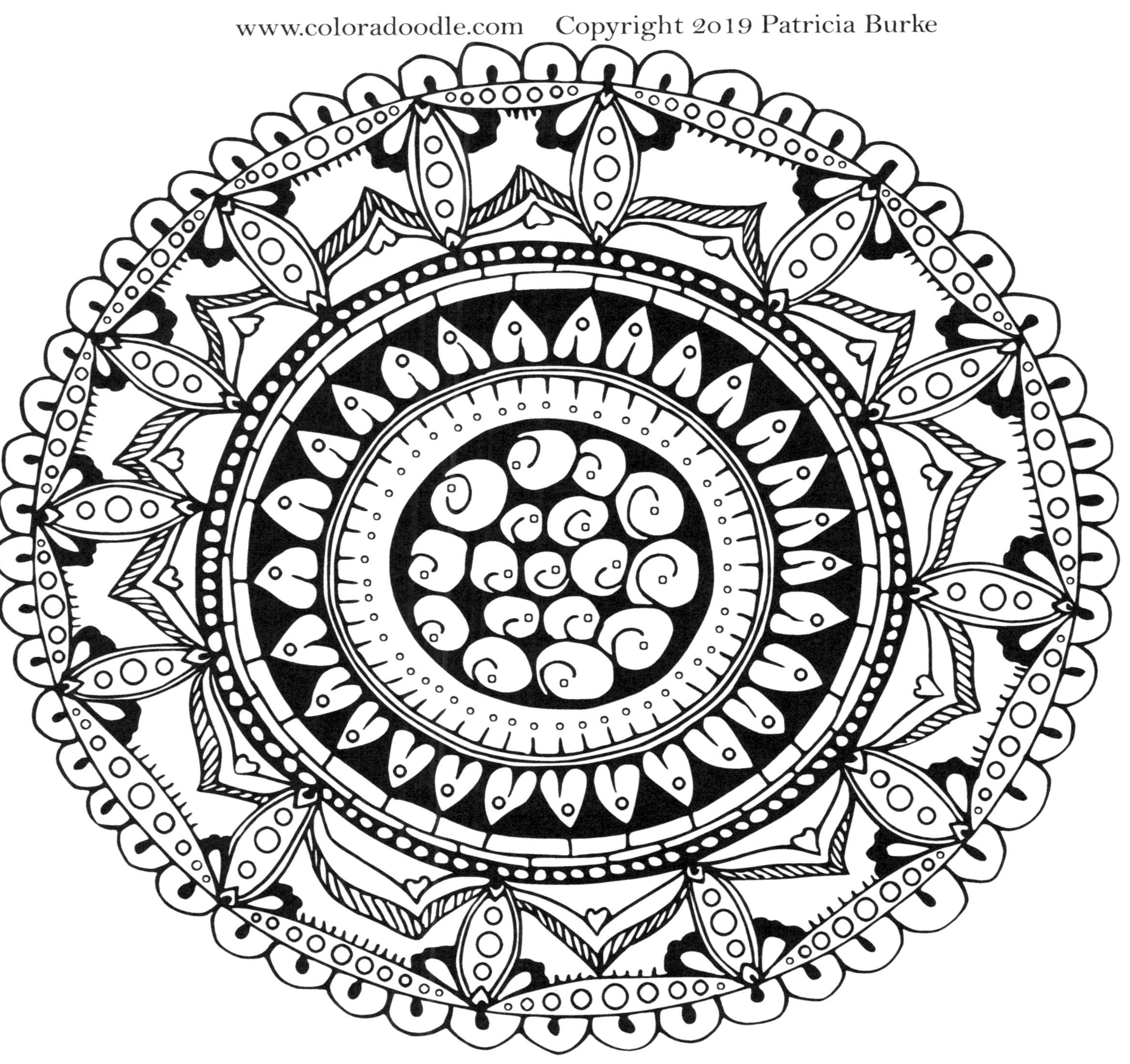

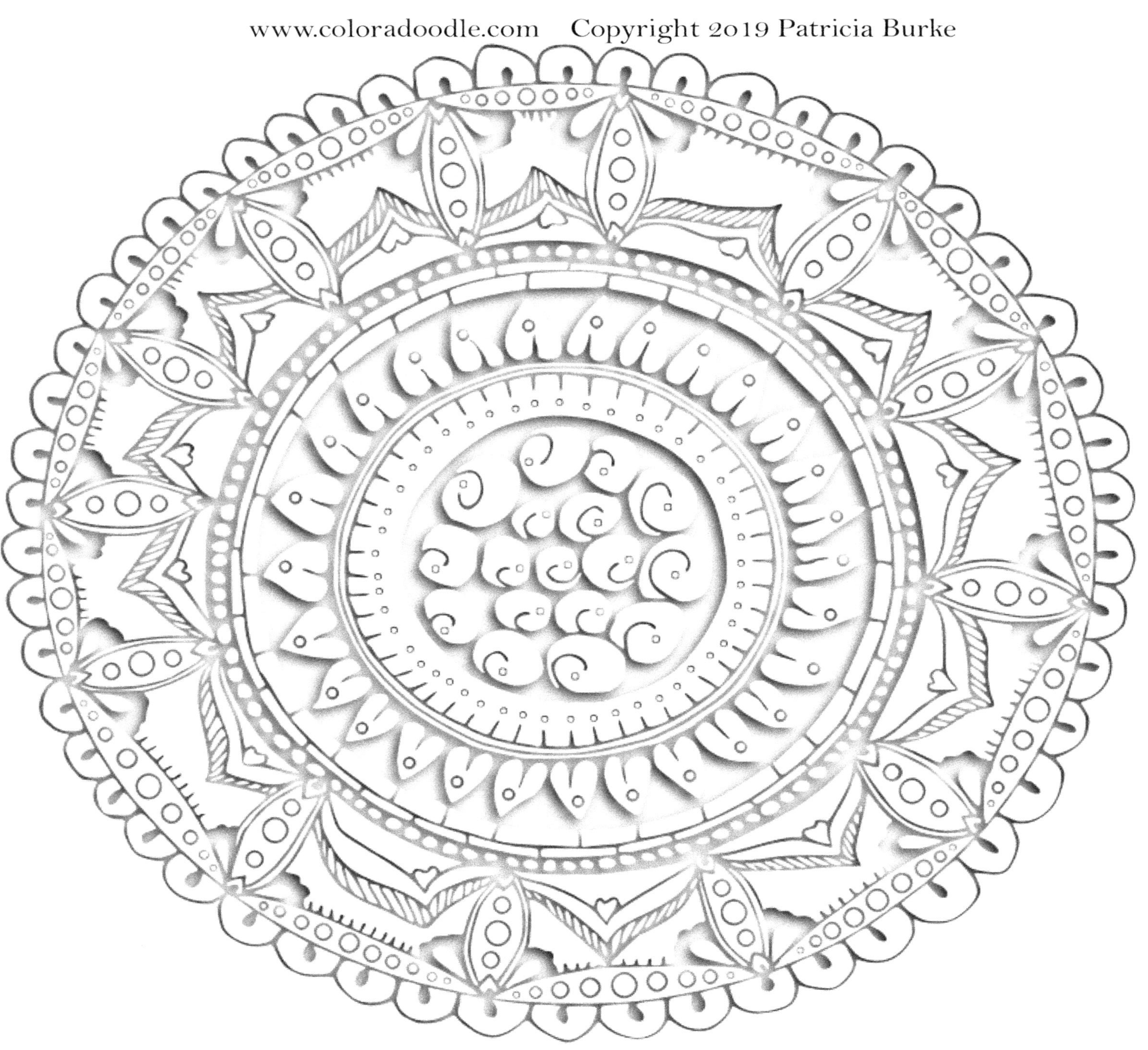

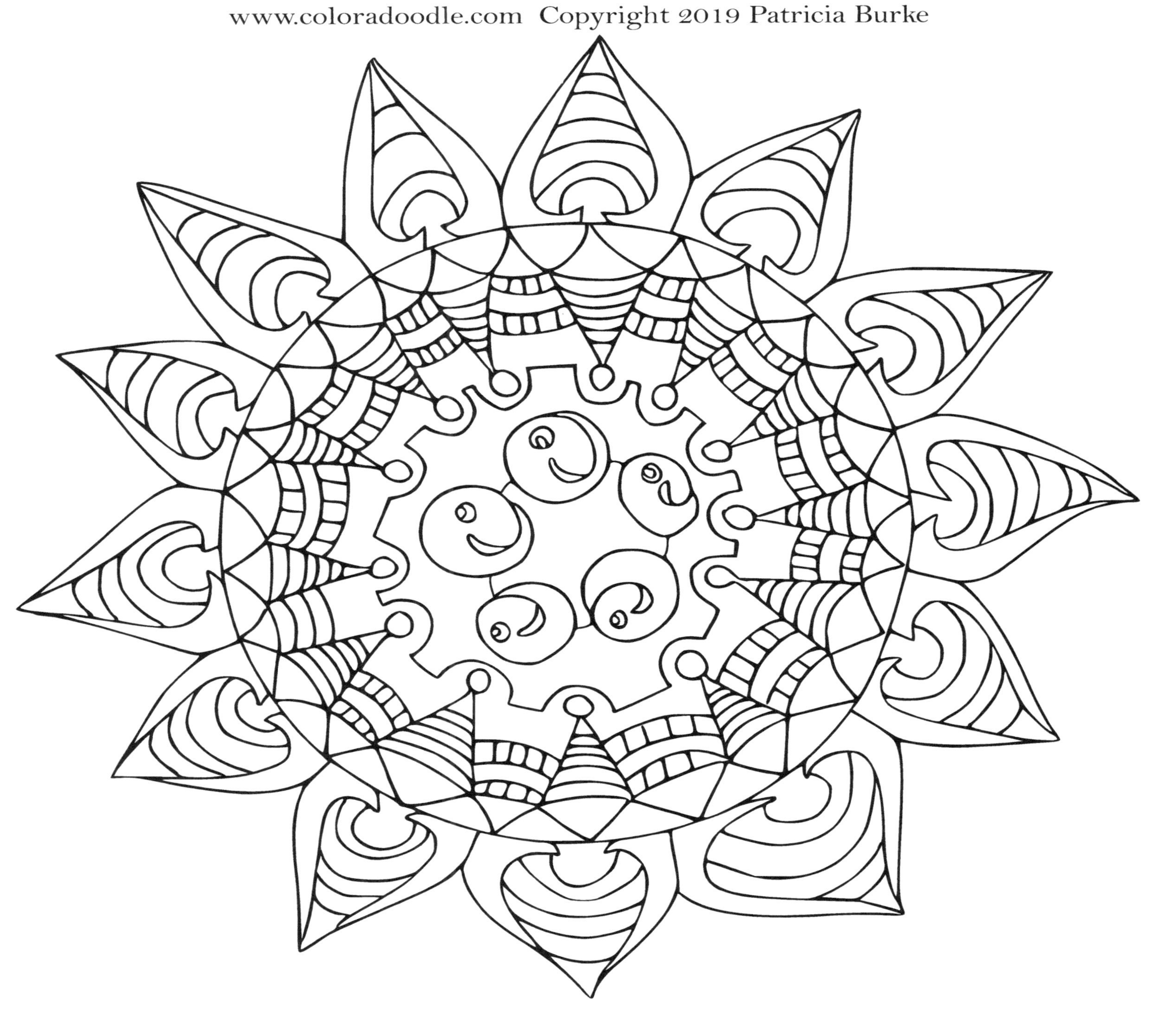

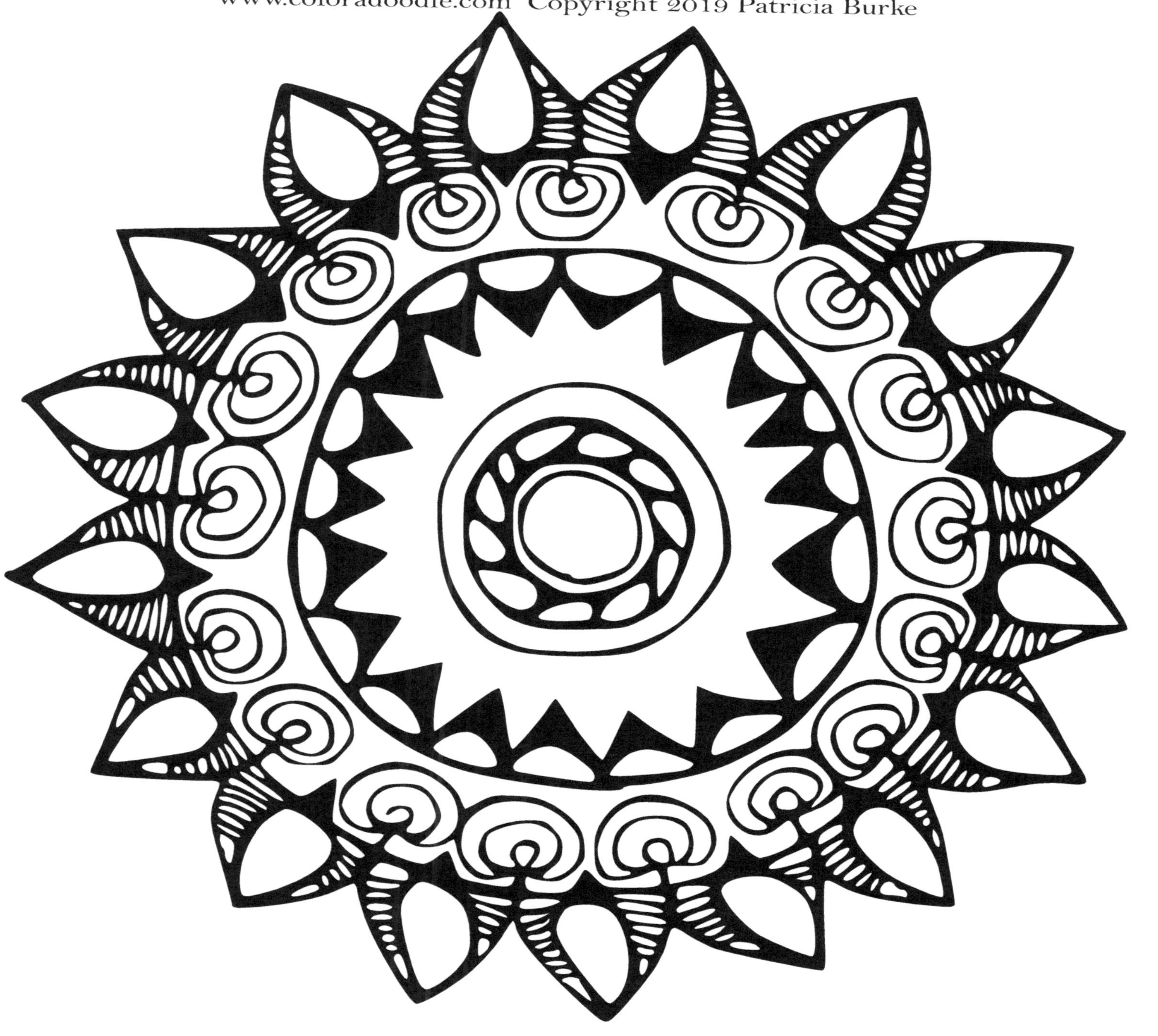

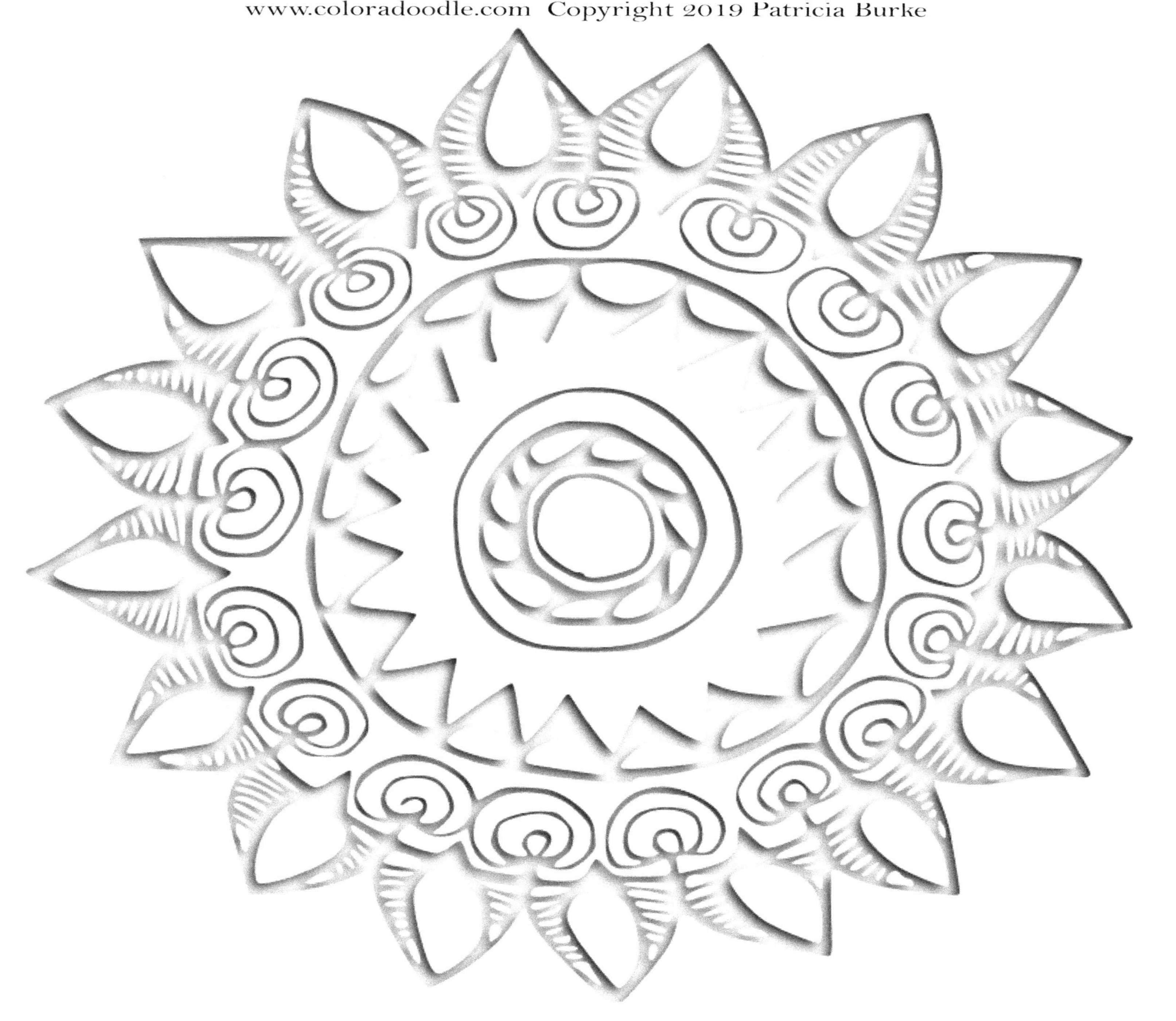

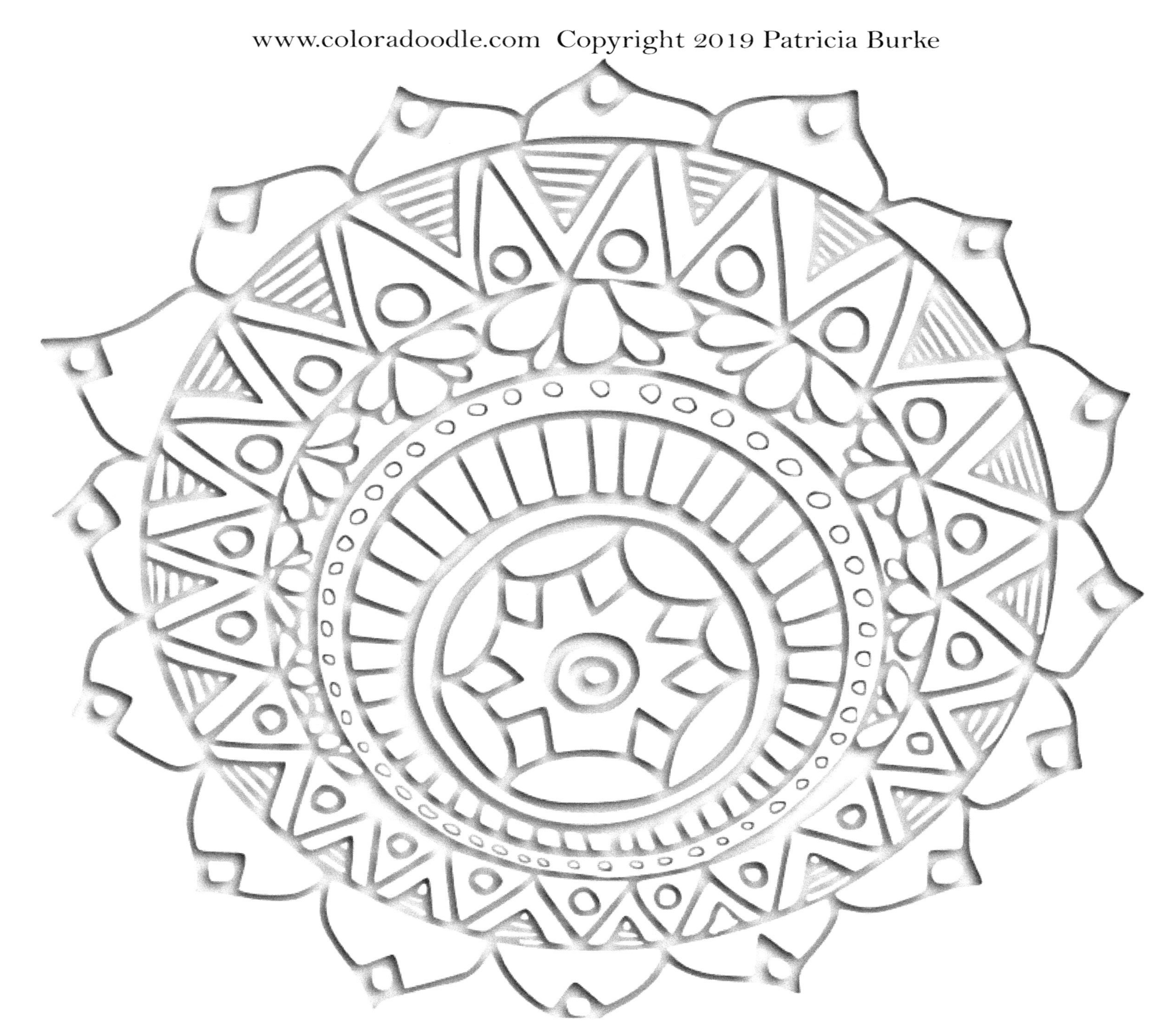

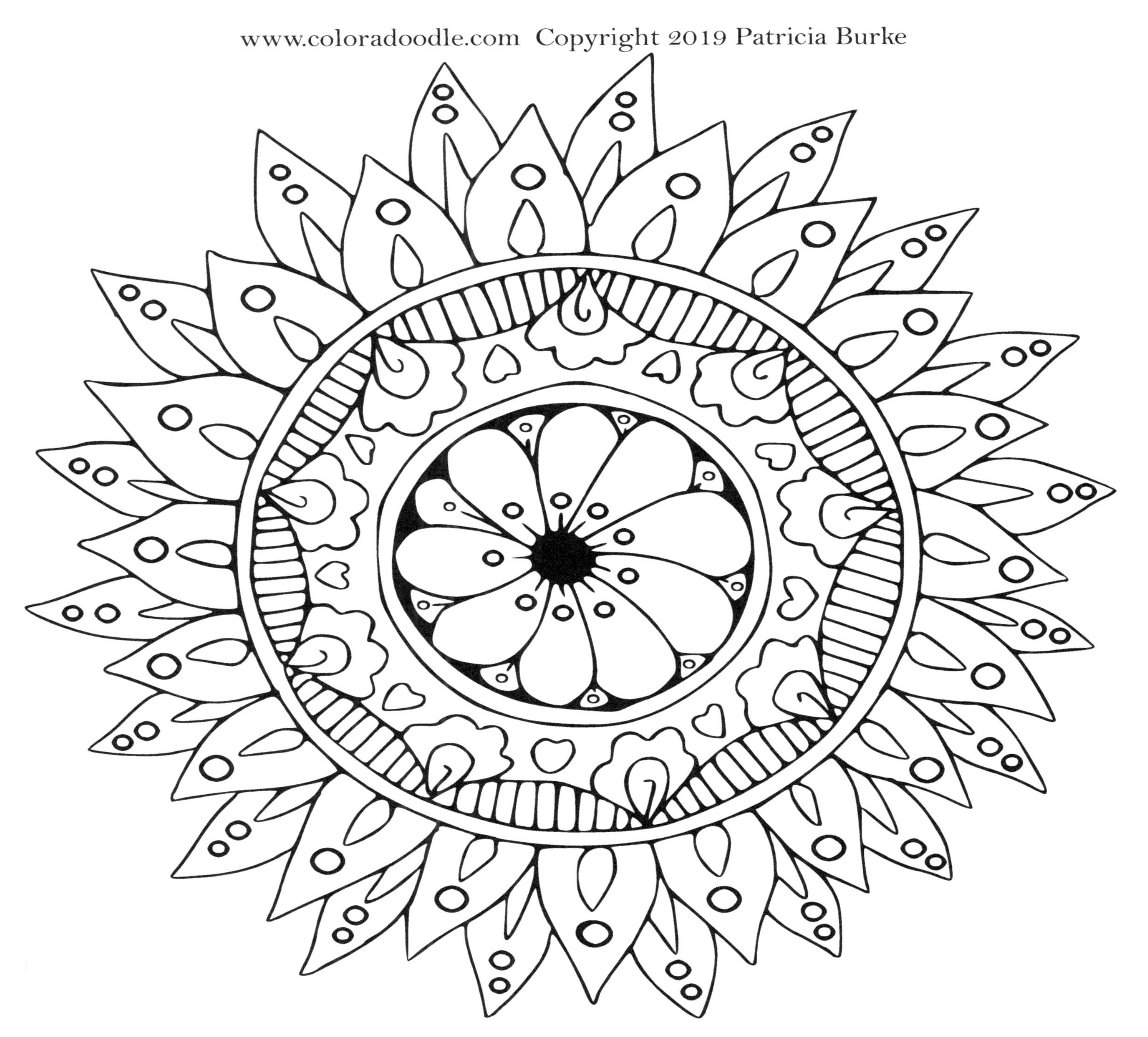

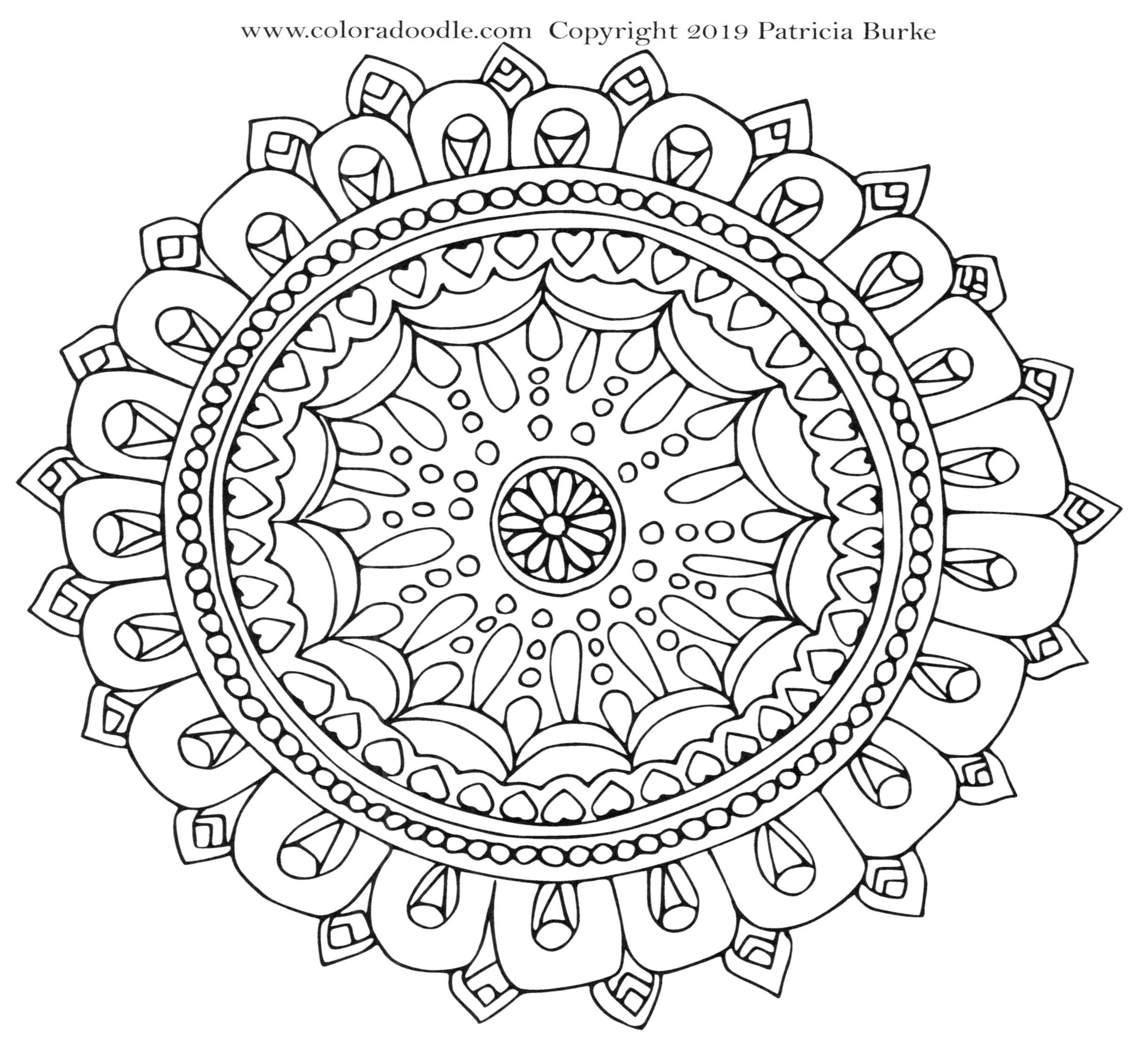

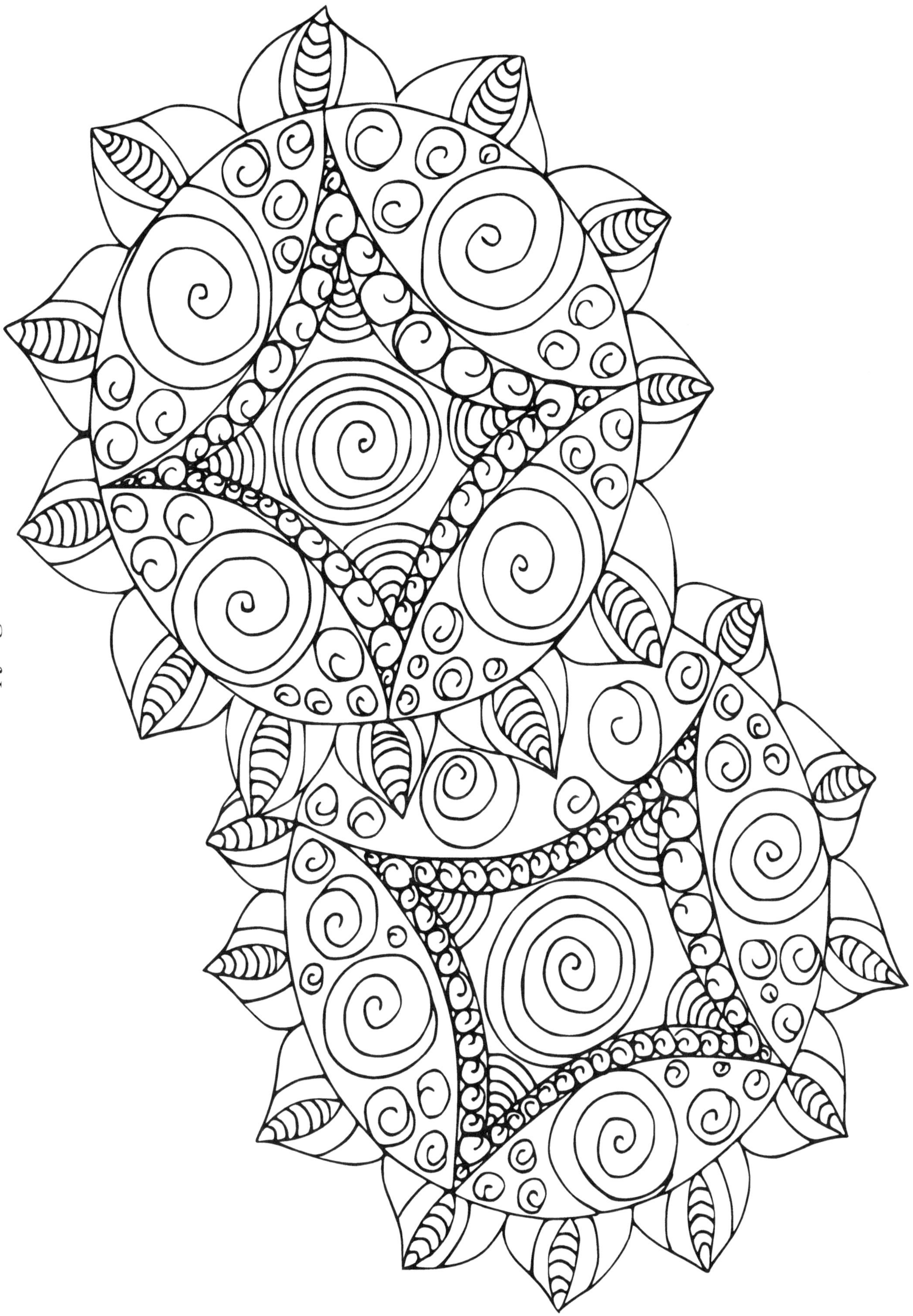

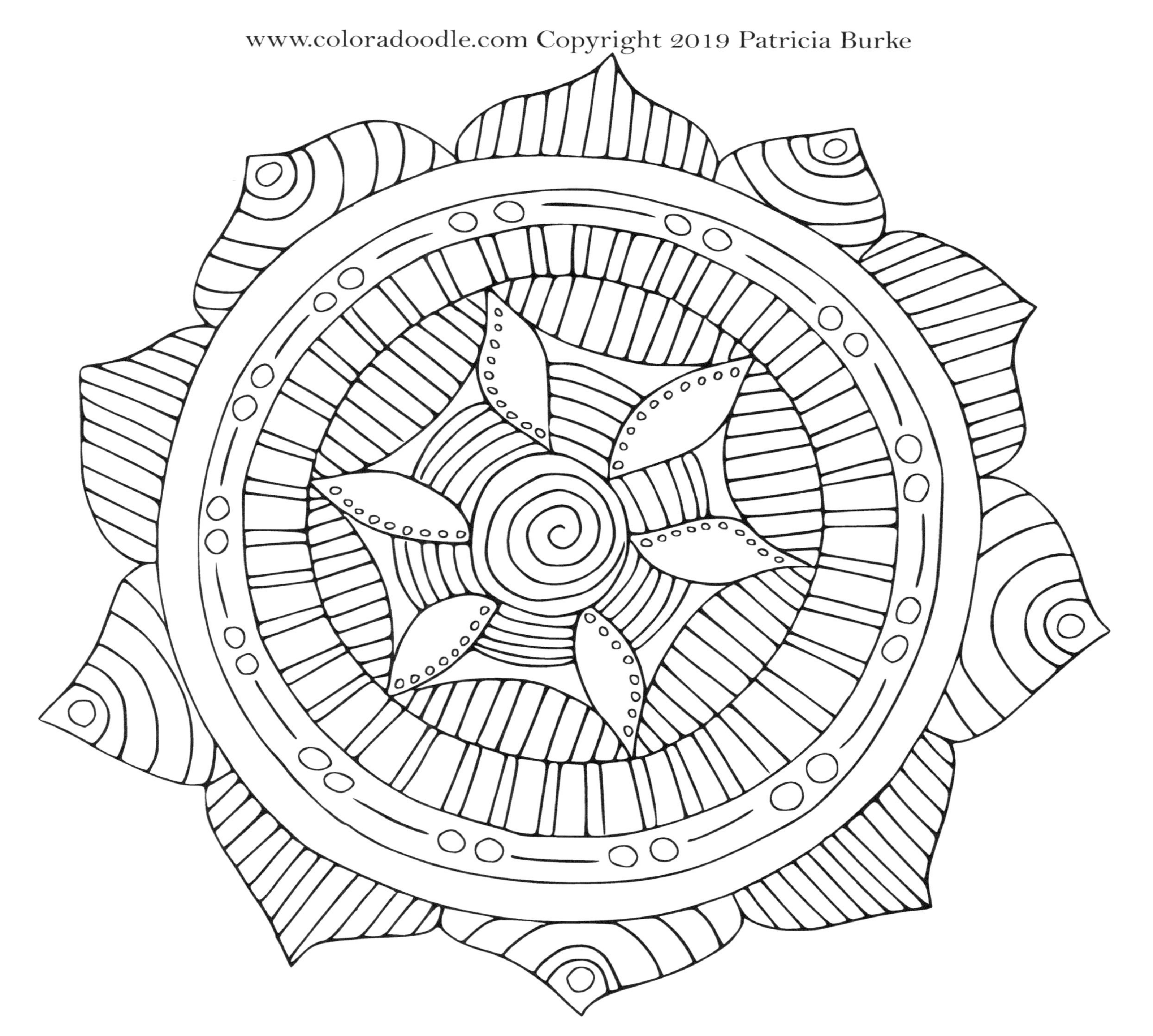

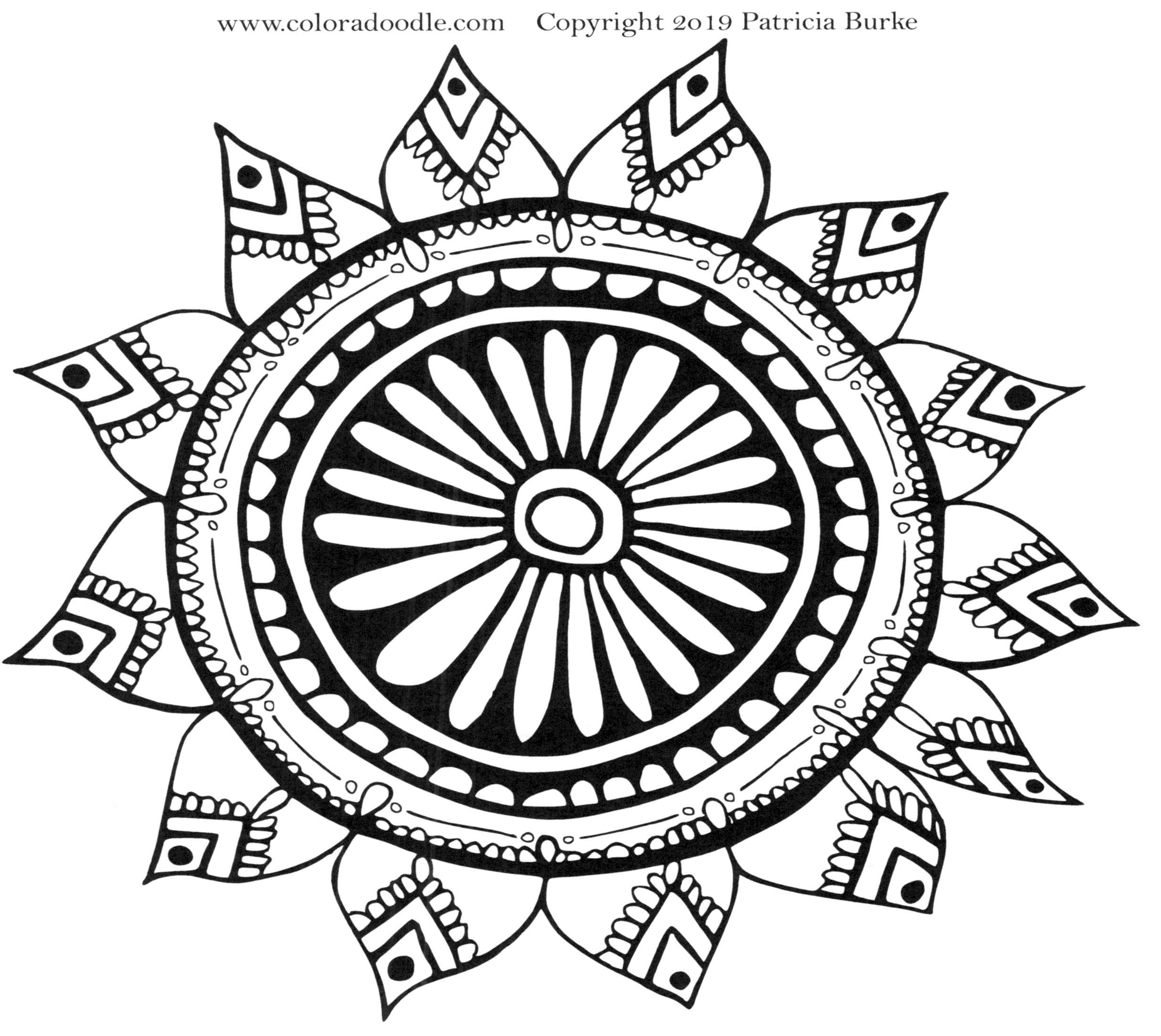

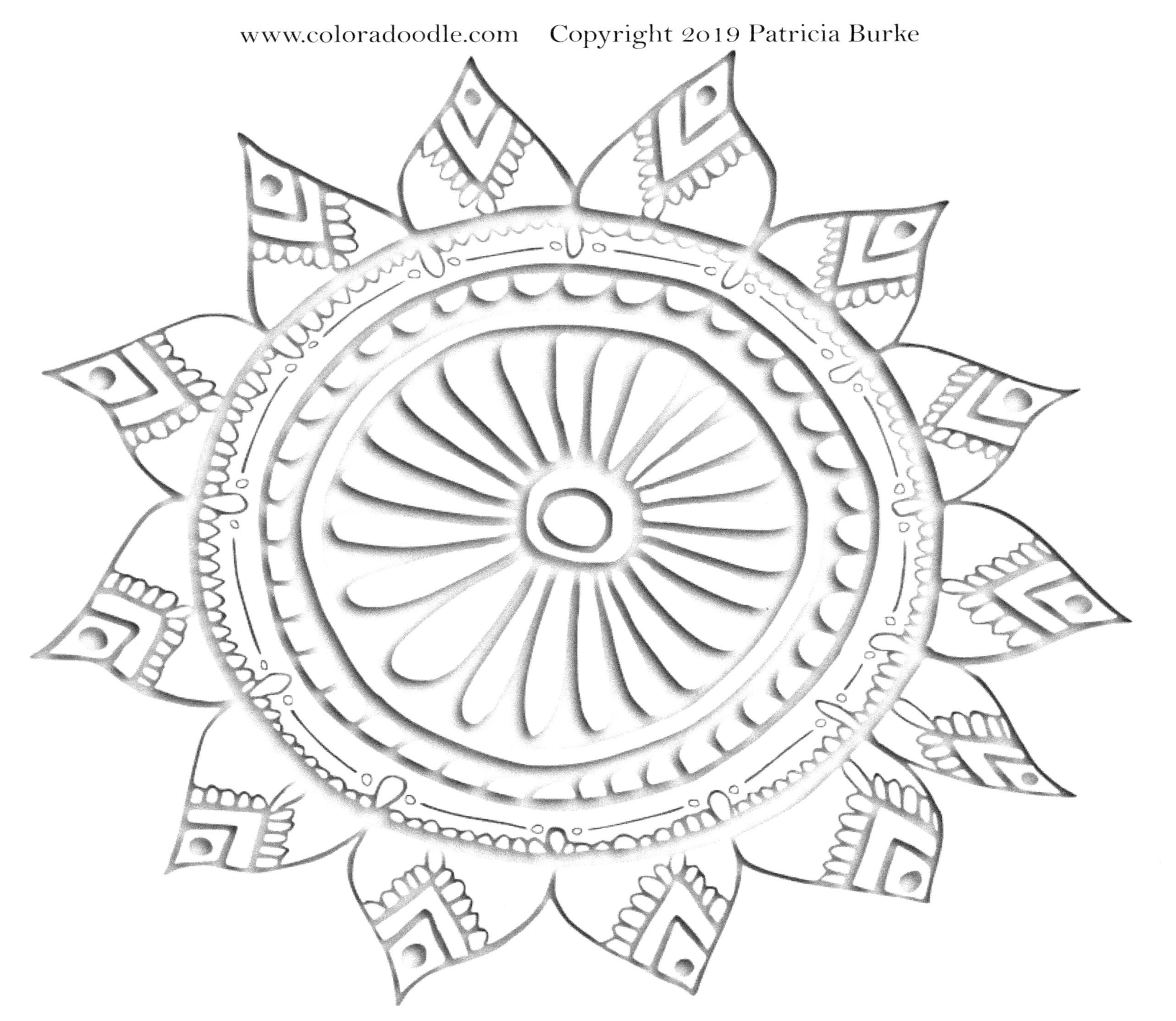

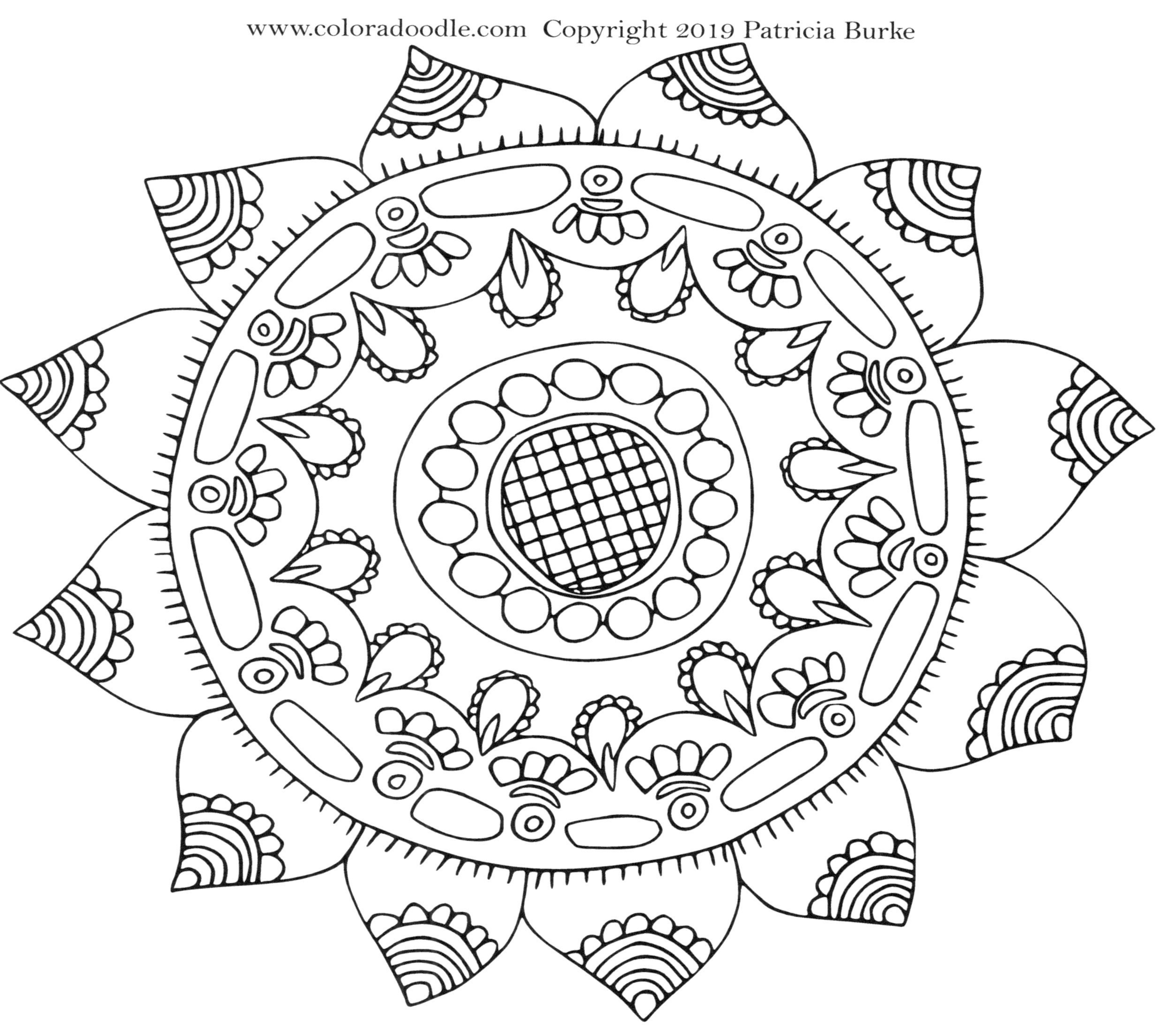

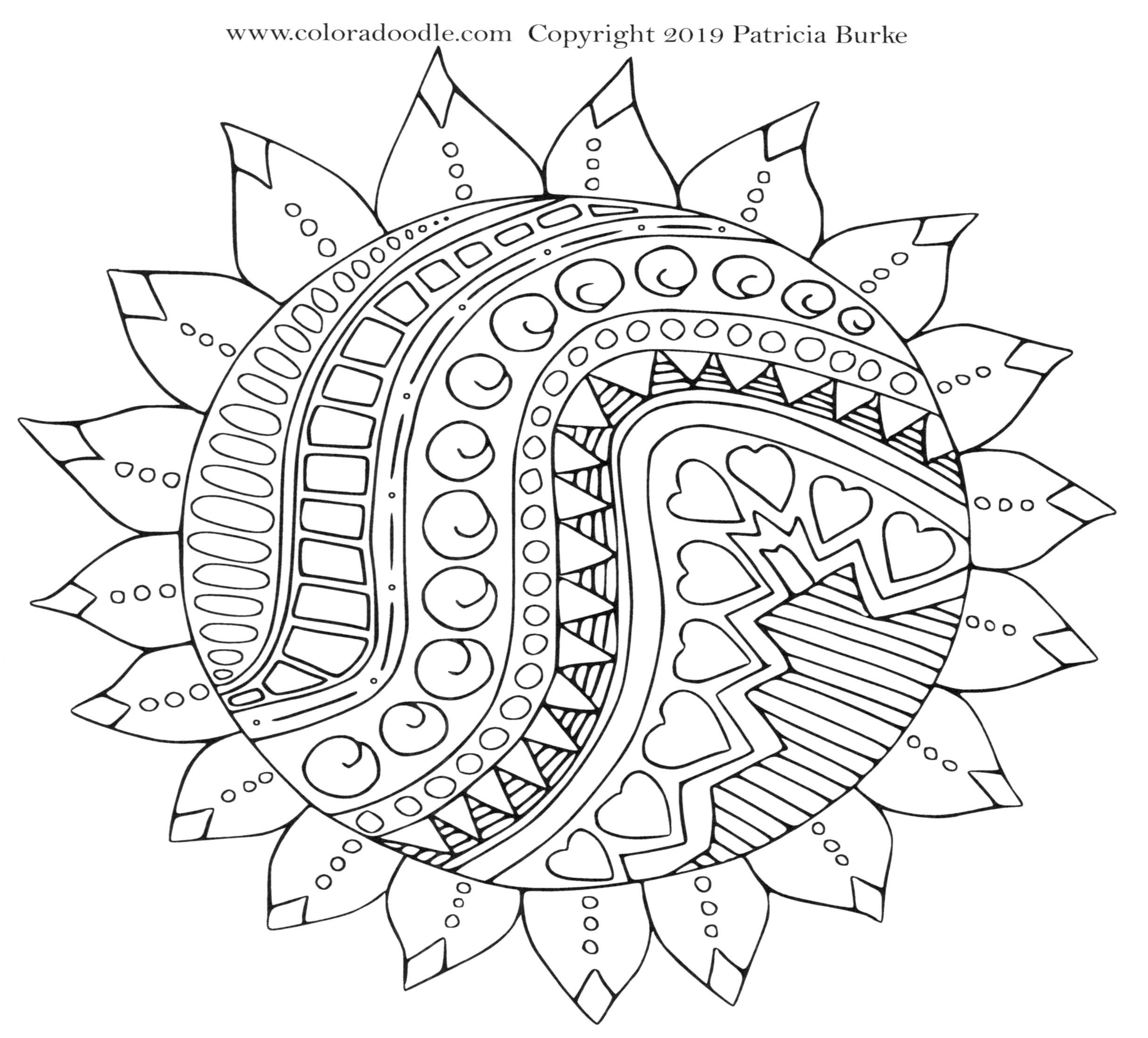

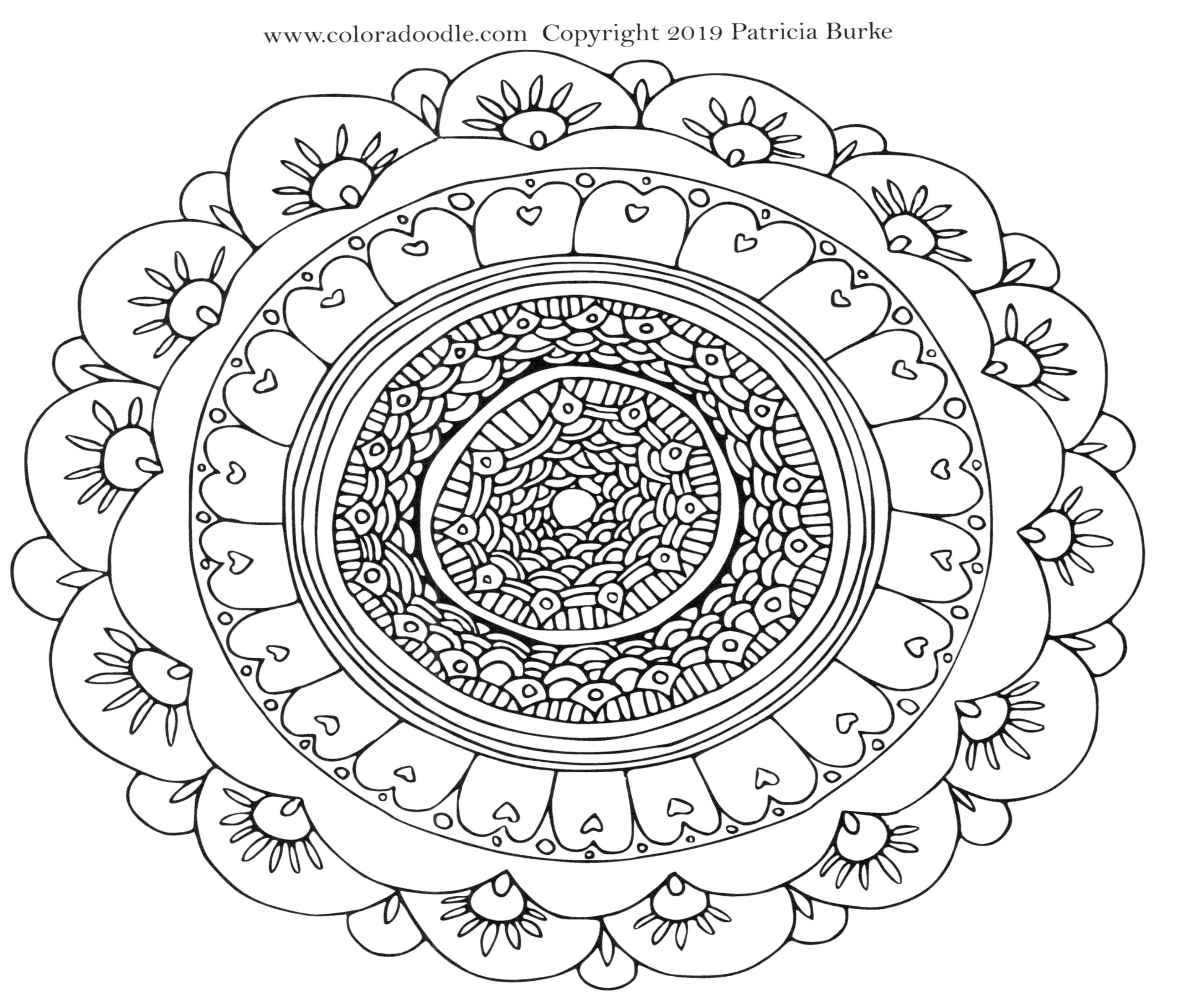

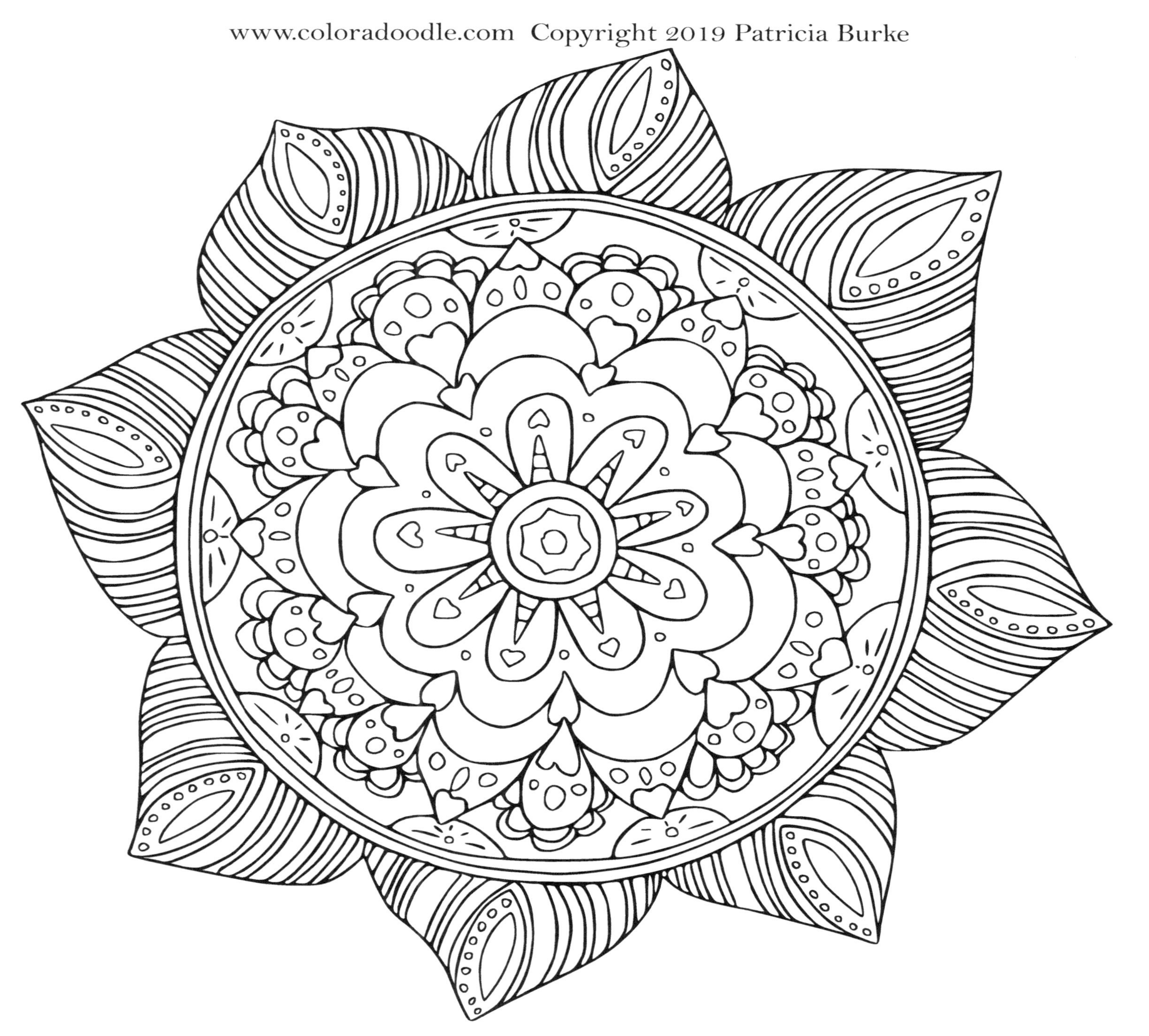

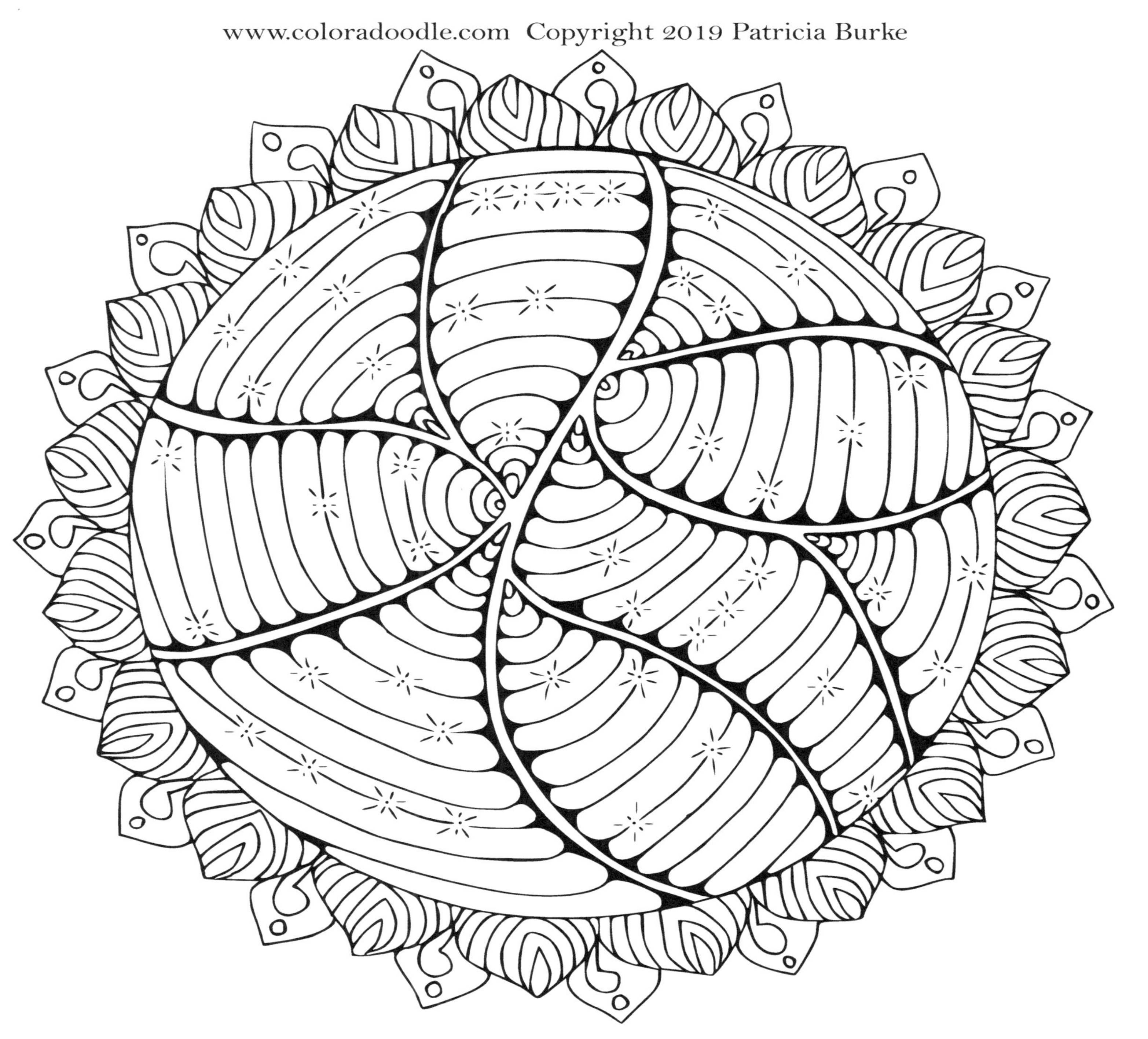

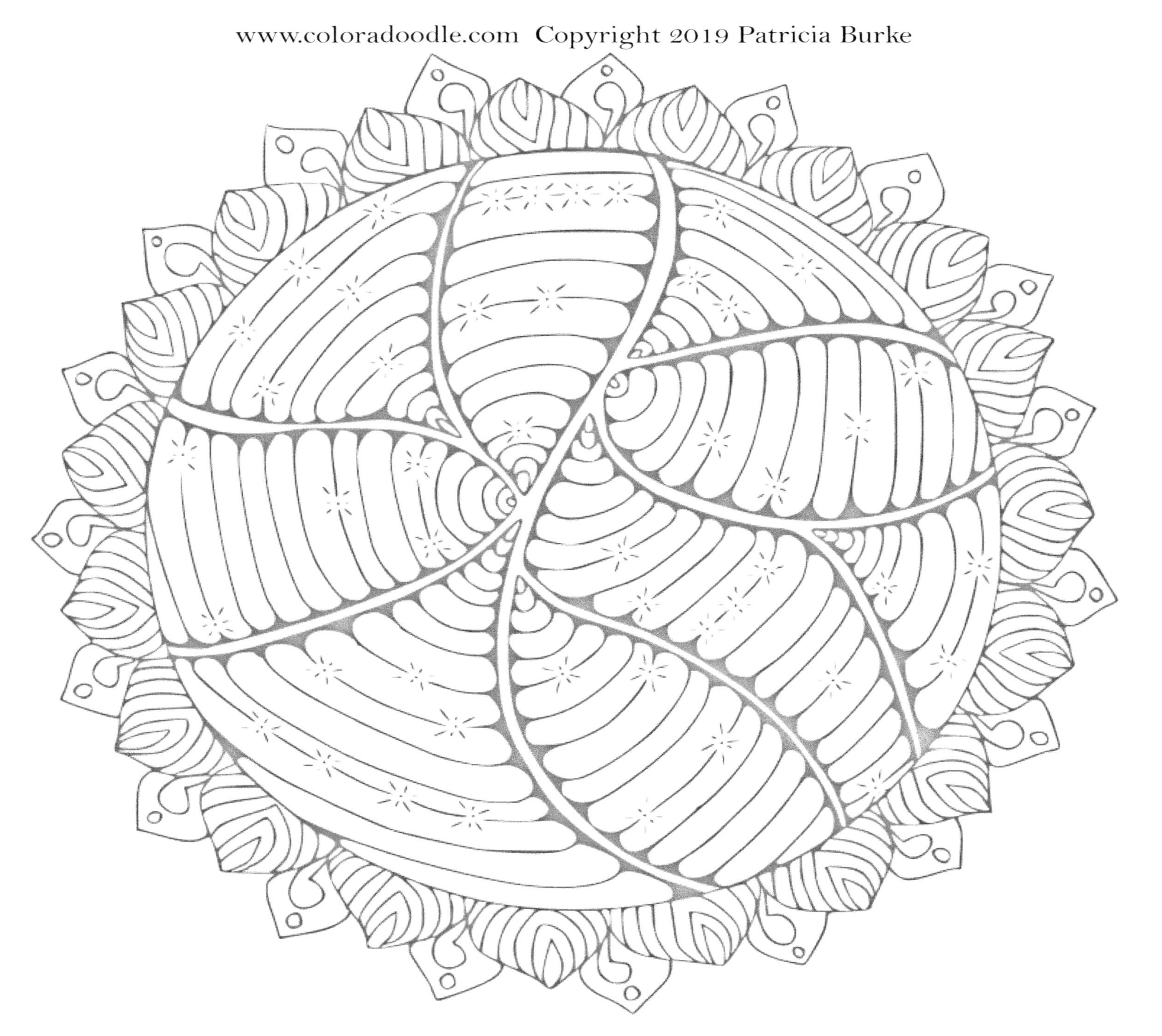

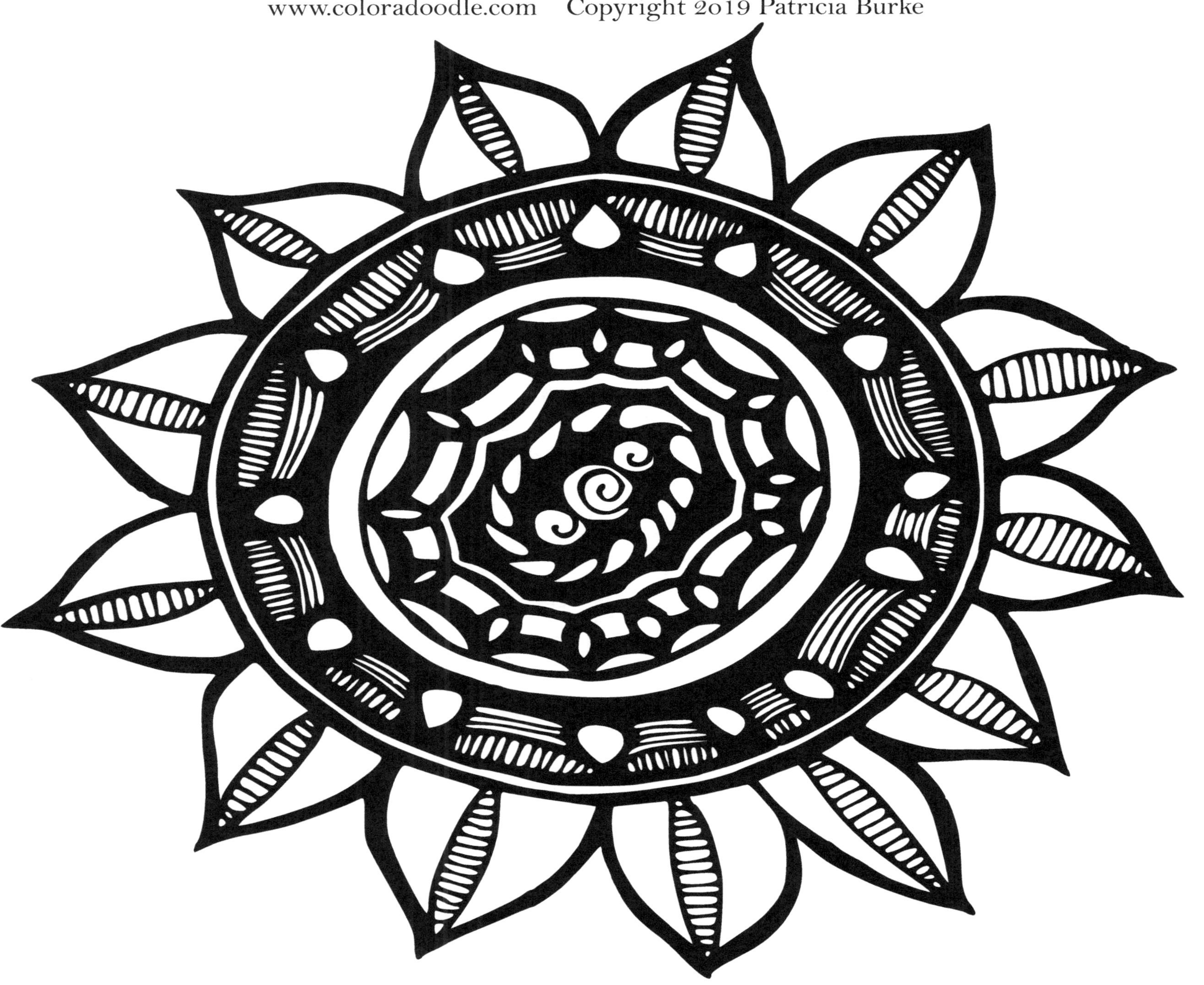

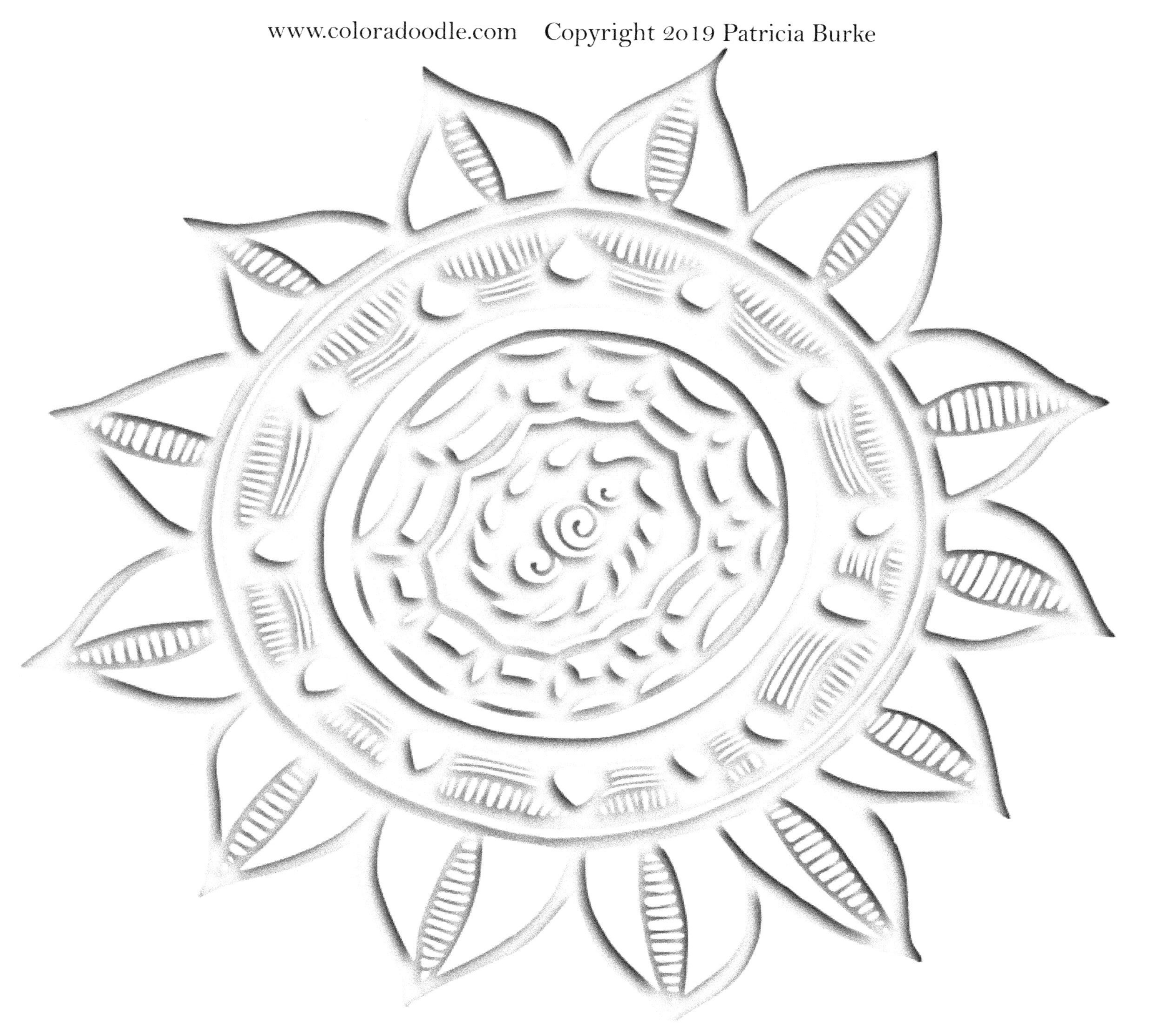

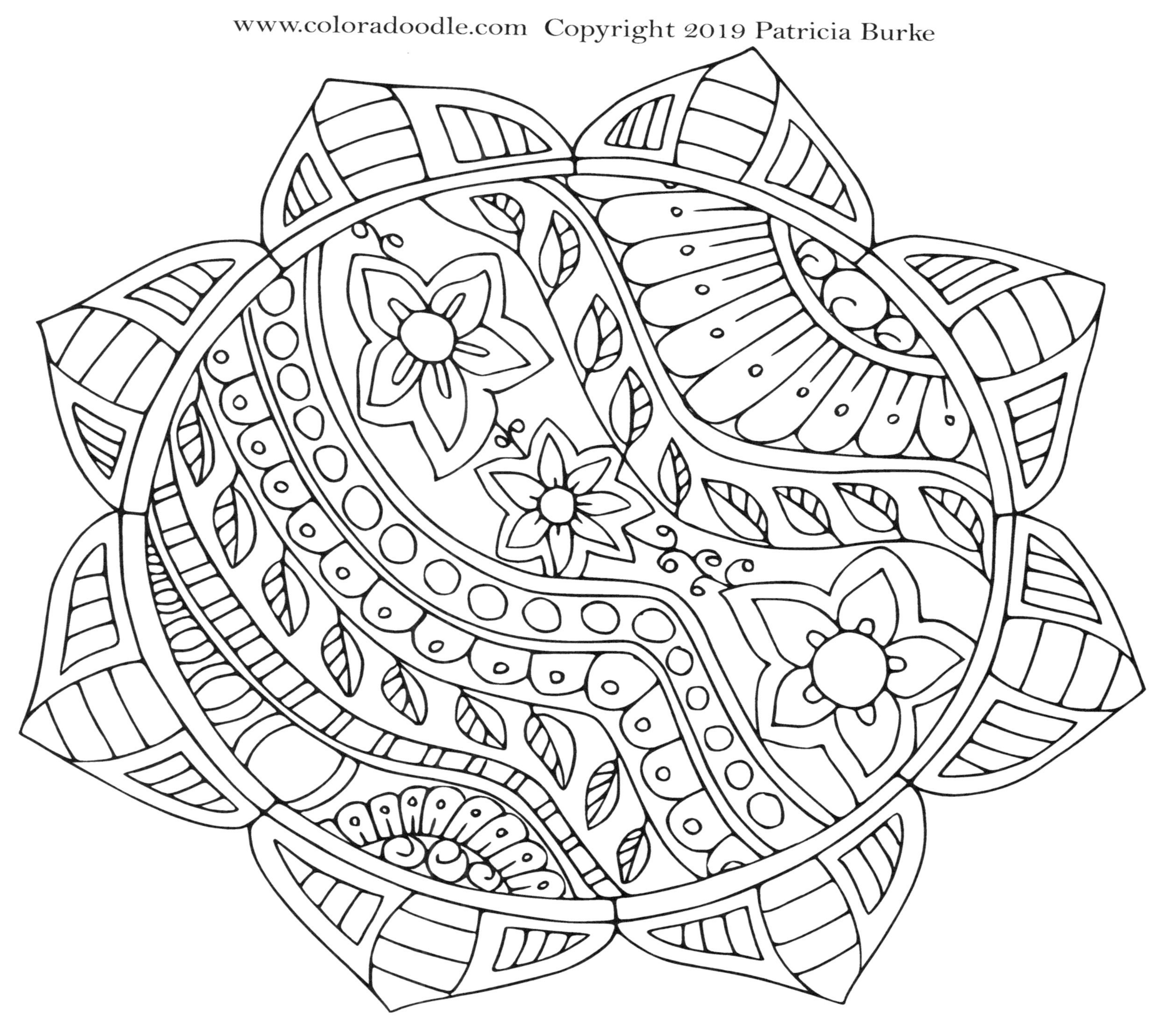

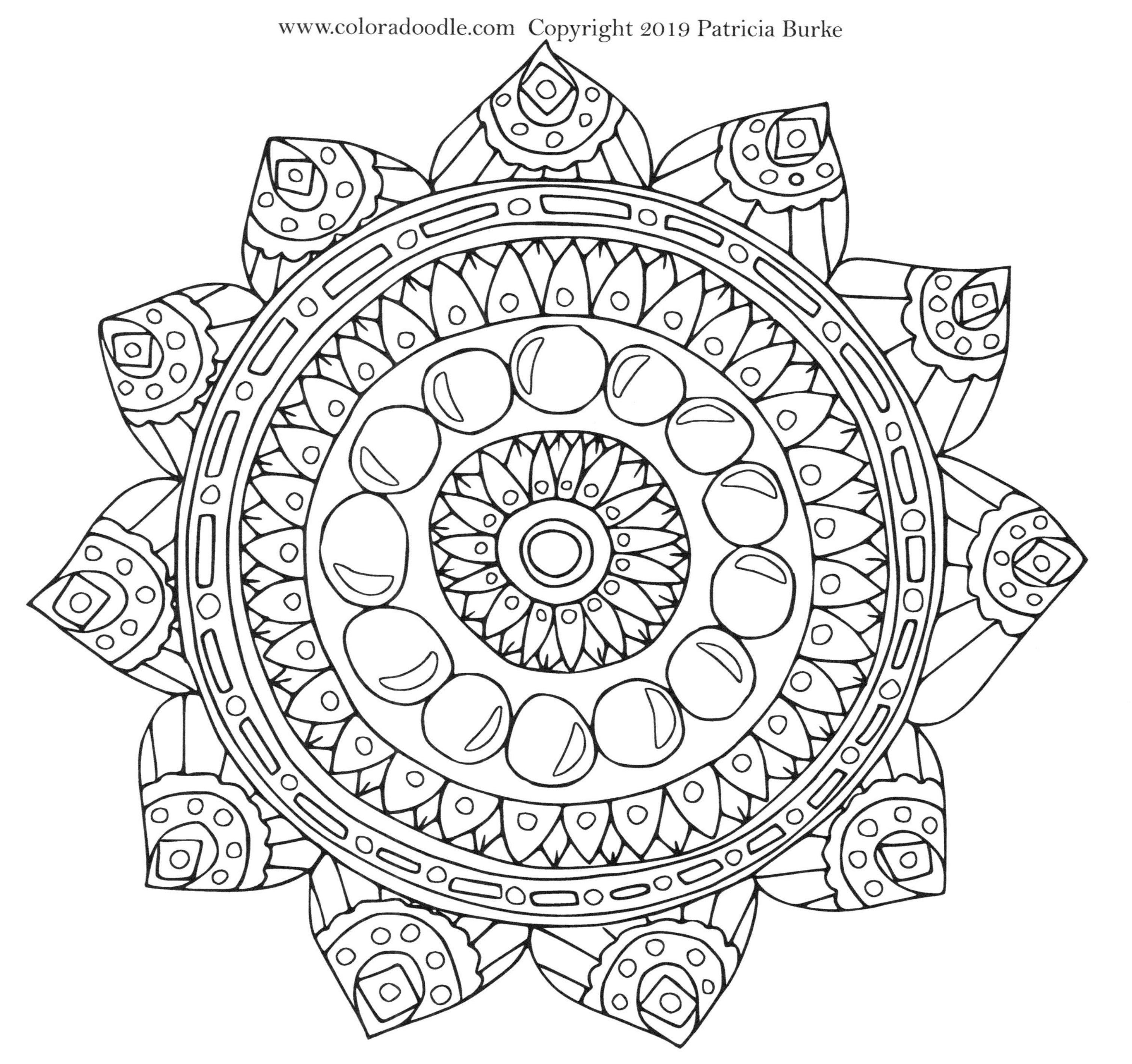

SUNFLOWERS
COLORING BOOK

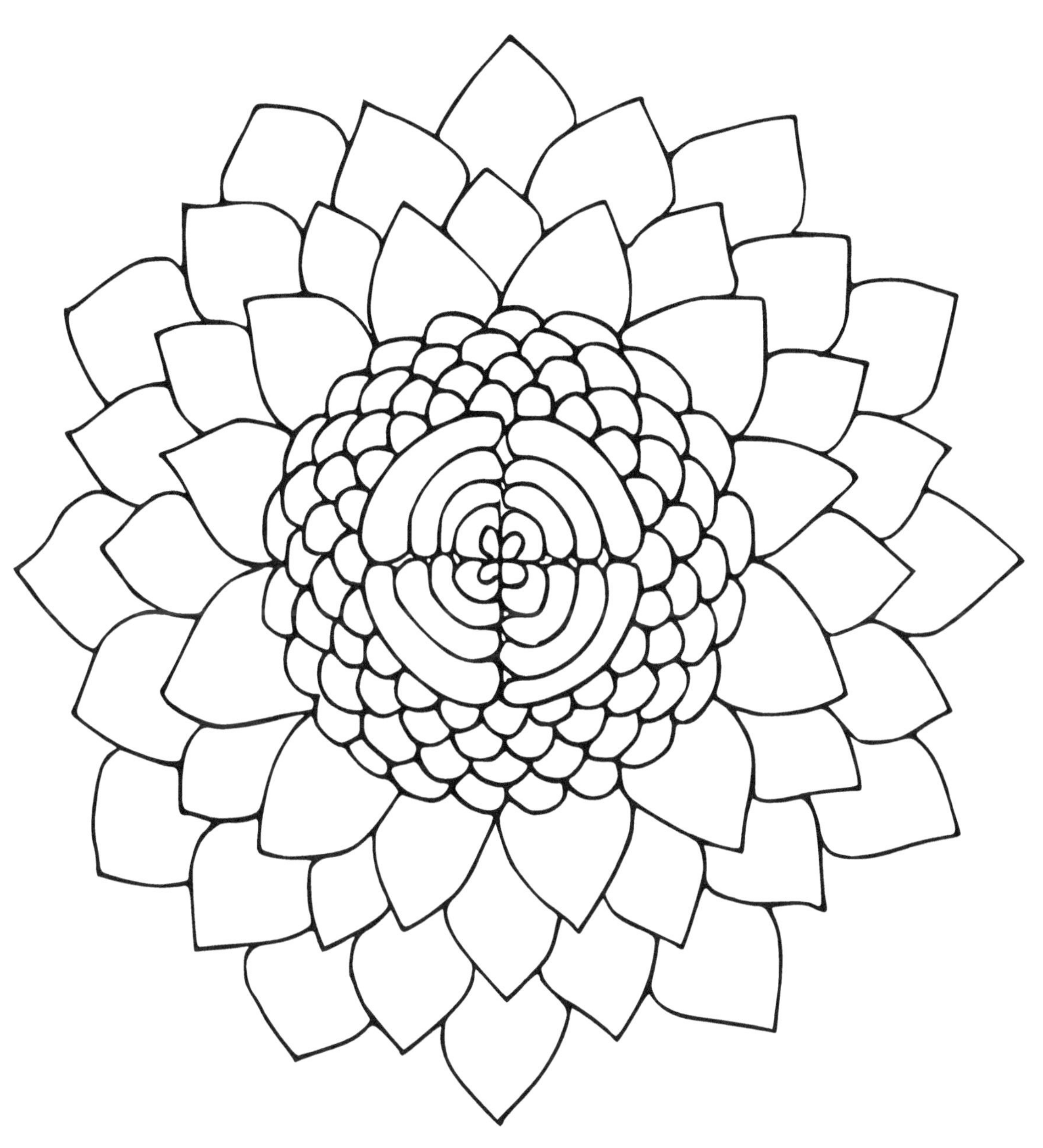

PATRICIA BURKE

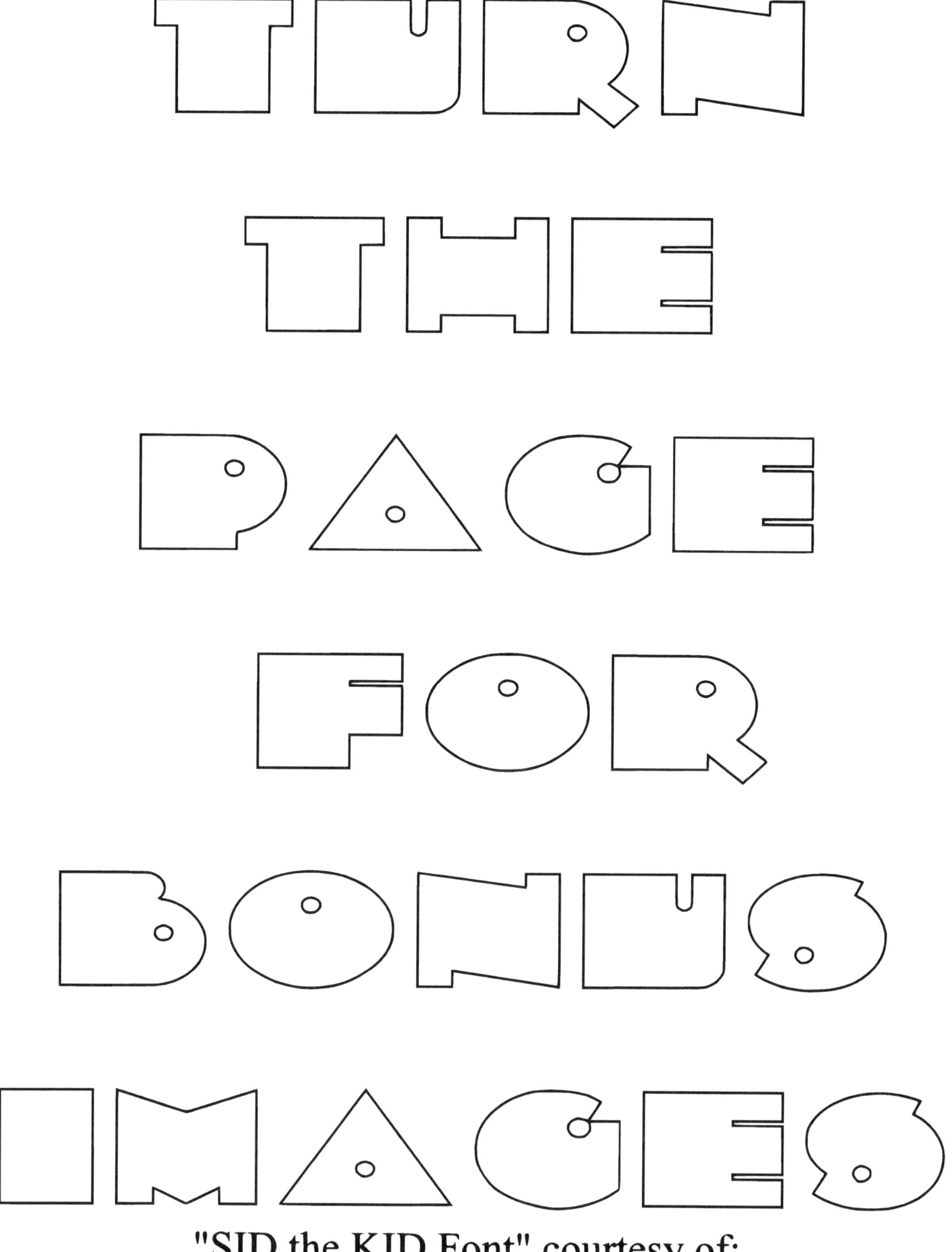

"SID the KID Font" courtesy of:
www.1001fonts.com

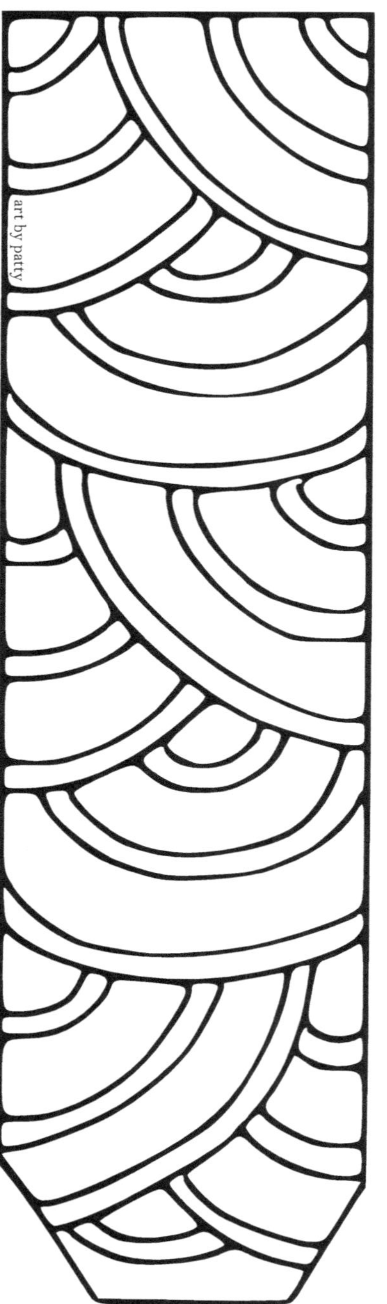

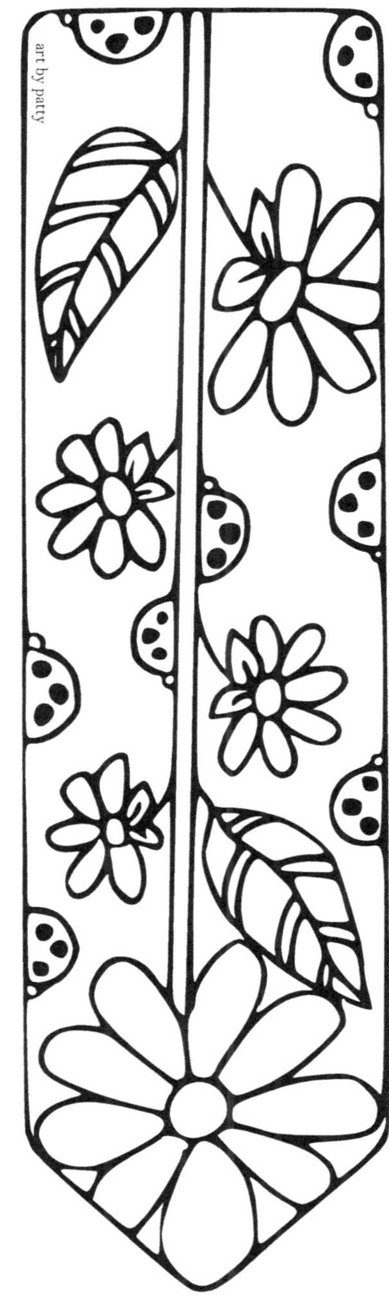

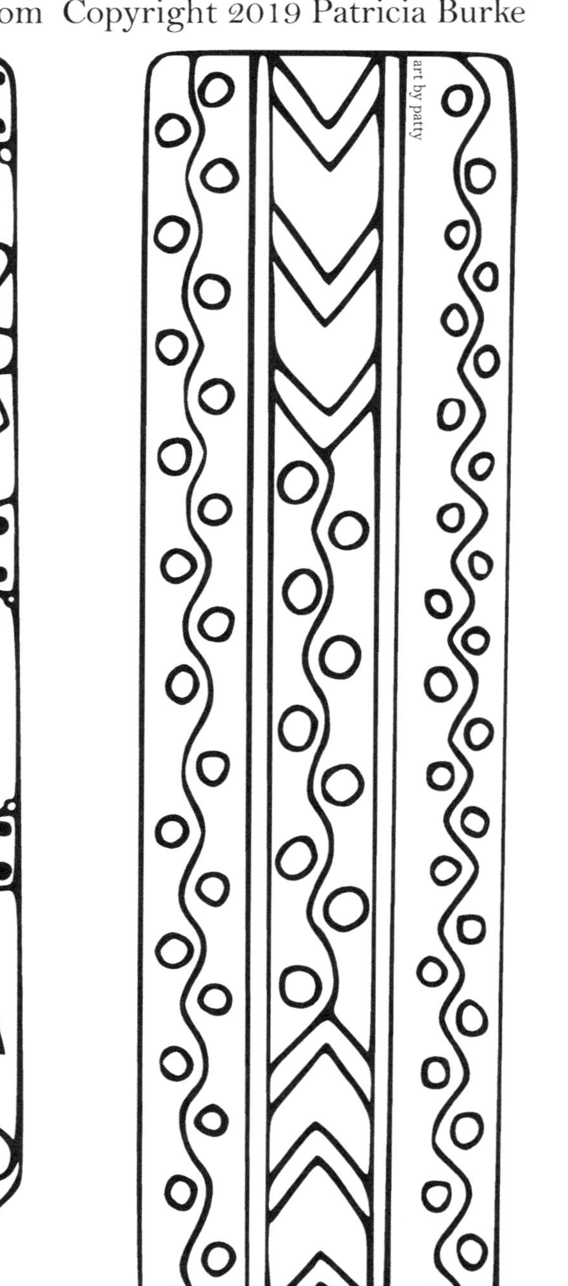

art by patty

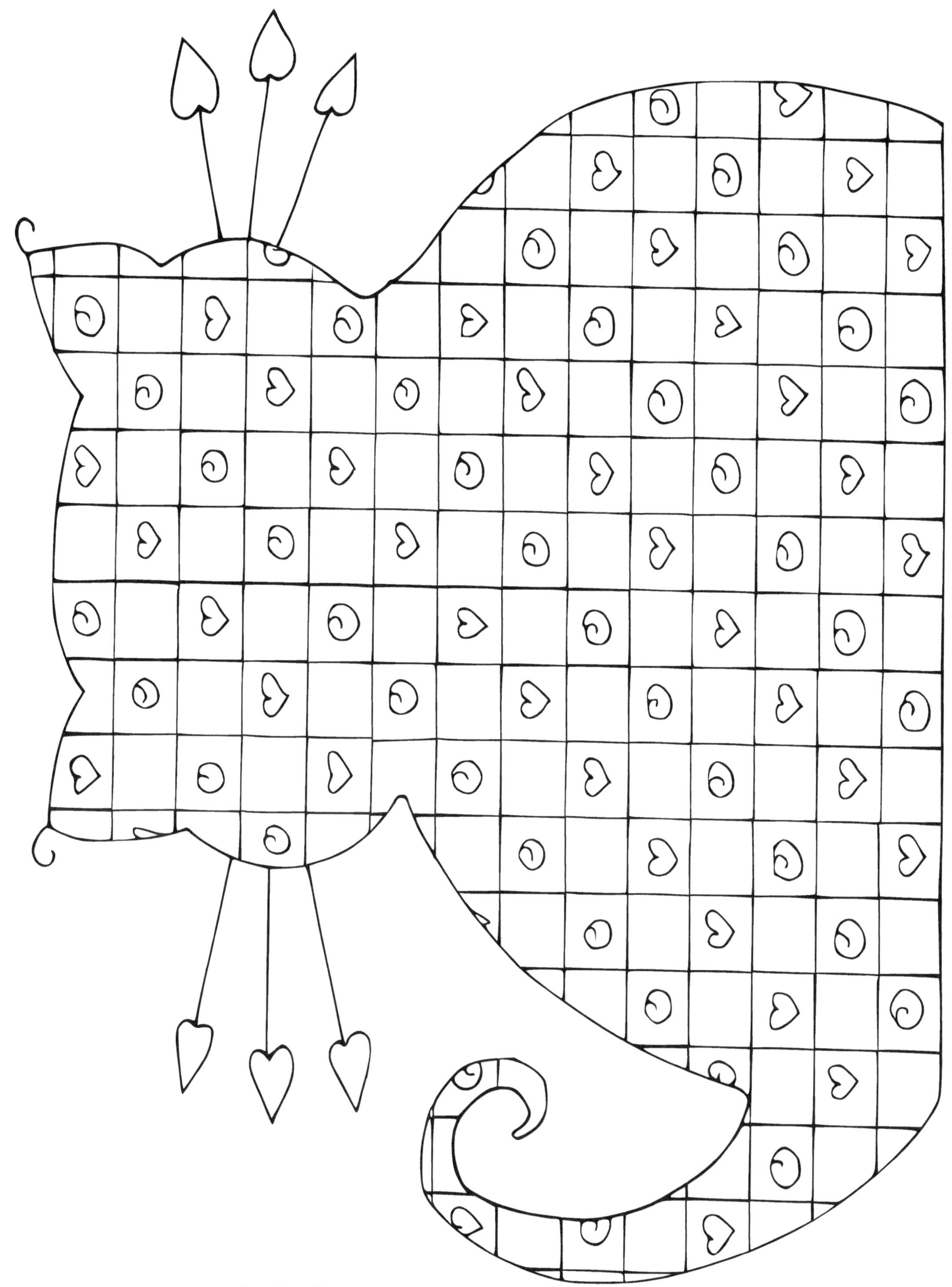

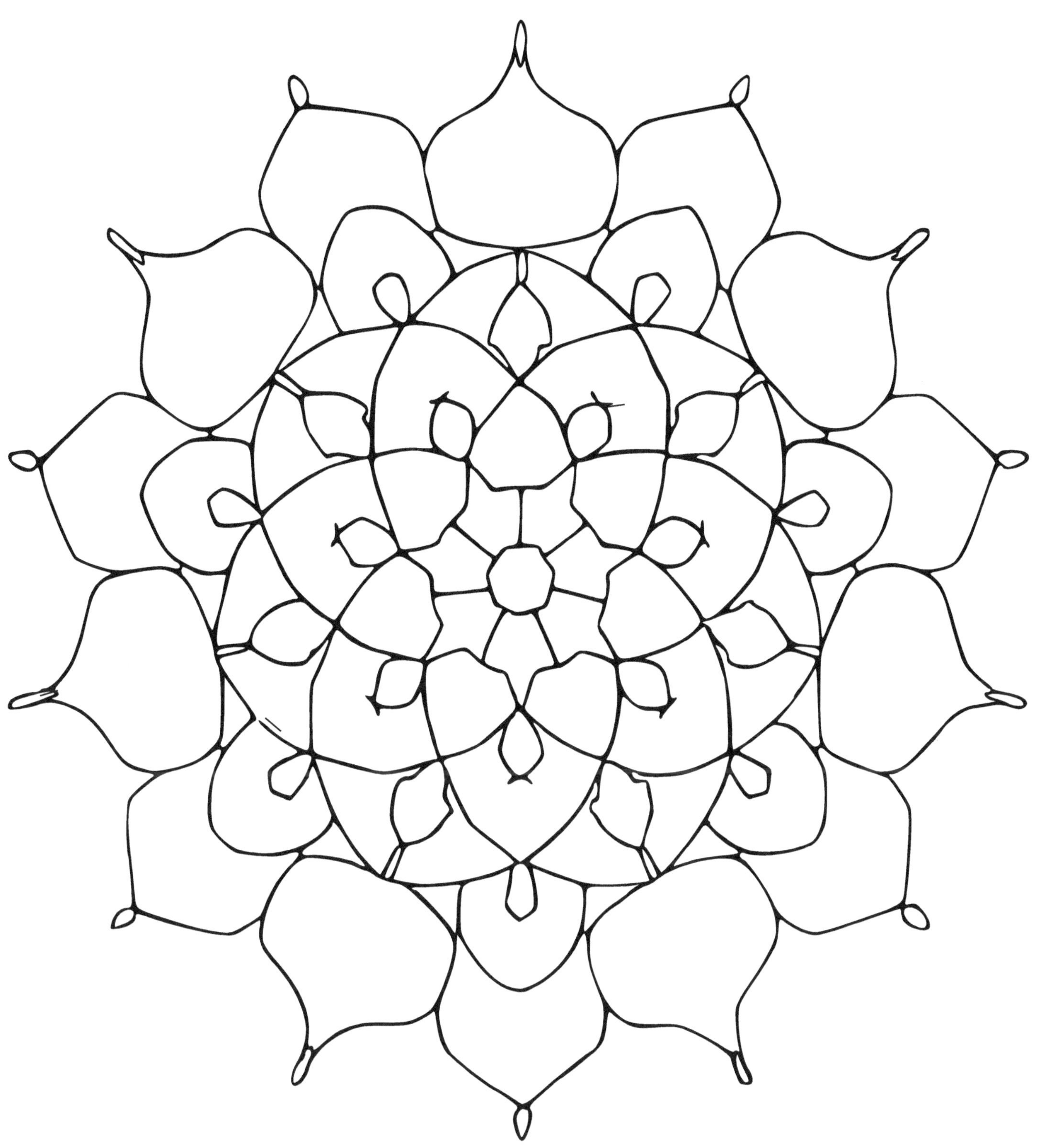

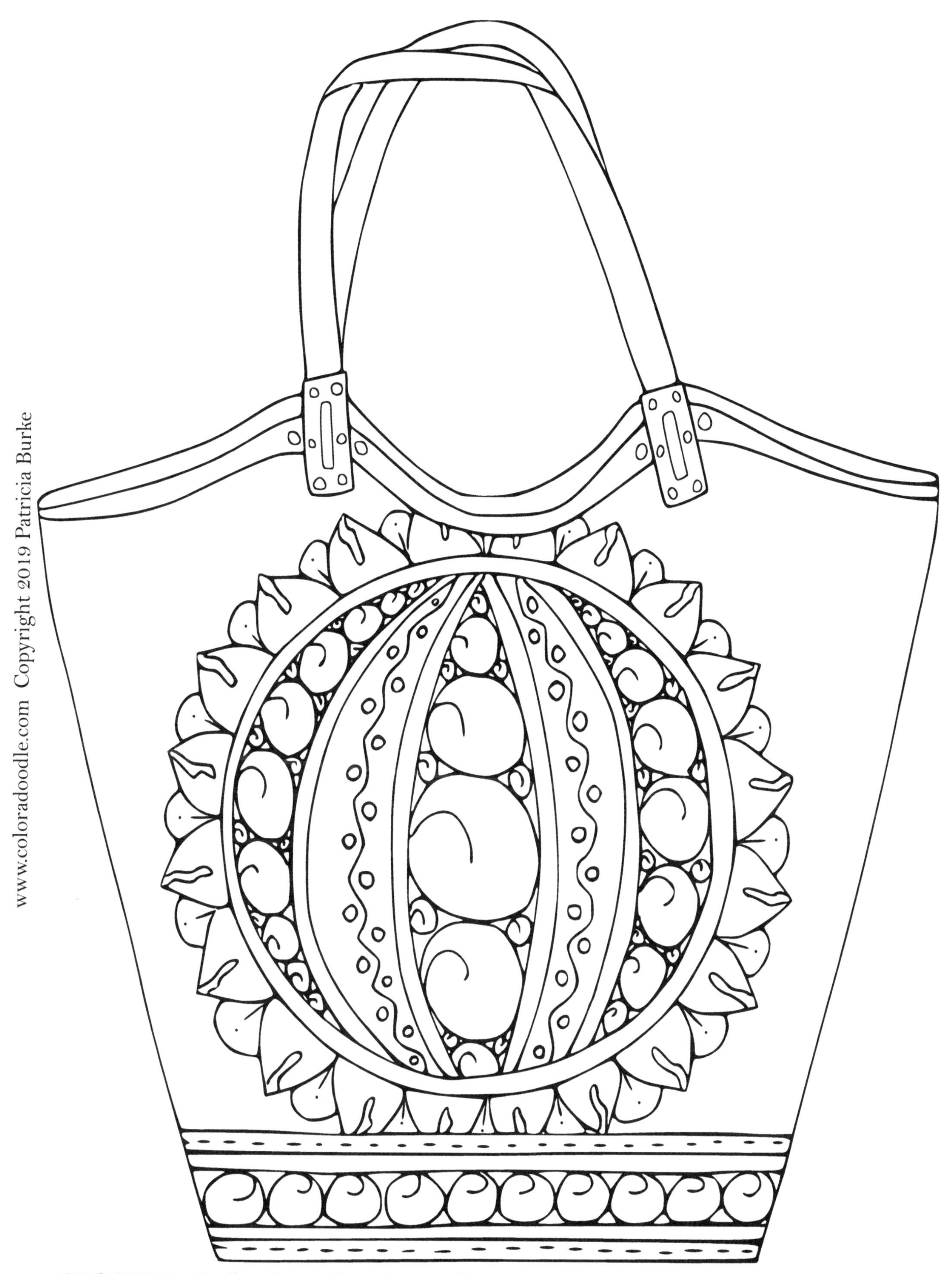

TOTES Coloring Book by Patricia Burke, coming soon

www.ingramcontent.com/pod-product-compliance
Lightning Source LLC
LaVergne TN
LVHW080924110826
845155LV00039B/201
9781951576011